TWENTIETH CENTURY
INTERPRETATIONS
OF
A PASSAGE TO INDIA

TWENTIETH CENTURY INTERPRETATIONS

OF

A PASSAGE
TO INDIA

A Collection of Critical Essays

Edited by
ANDREW RUTHERFORD

Prentice-Hall, Inc.   A SPECTRUM BOOK *Englewood Cliffs, N. J.*

Quotations from *A Passage to India* by E. M. Forster are used
by permission of Edward Arnold (Publishers) Ltd.

Copyright © 1970 by Prentice-Hall, Inc., Englewood Cliffs, New Jersey. A SPEC-
TRUM BOOK. All rights reserved. No part of this book may be reproduced in
any form or by any means without permission in writing from the publisher.
C–13-652693-4; P–13-652685-3. *Library of Congress Catalog Card Number 75-120797.*
Printed in the United States of America.

Current printing (last number):
10 9 8 7 6 5 4 3 2 1

PRENTICE-HALL INTERNATIONAL, INC. (*London*)
PRENTICE-HALL OF AUSTRALIA, PTY. LTD. (*Sydney*)
PRENTICE-HALL OF CANADA, LTD. (*Toronto*)
PRENTICE-HALL OF INDIA PRIVATE LIMITED (*New Delhi*)
PRENTICE-HALL OF JAPAN, INC. (*Tokyo*)

This volume is meant to be used in conjunction with Malcolm Bradbury, ed., *Forster: A Collection of Critical Essays* (Englewood Cliffs, N. J.: Prentice-Hall, Inc., 1966), and the essays reprinted here complement those in that collection.

Contents

TWENTIETH CENTURY
INTERPRETATIONS
OF

A PASSAGE TO INDIA

Introduction

by Andrew Rutherford

I

A Passage to India, generally acknowledged to be E. M. Forster's masterpiece, is at once a historical document, a philosophical statement, and a work of conscious literary art; and the best criticism of this novel has therefore focused on its political, ethical, and metaphysical implications, as well as on such features as its comedy and characterization, its symbolism, rhetorical organization, and aesthetic quality.

II

With the demise of the British Empire—more particularly since the granting of Indian independence in 1947 and the winds of change blowing through Africa in the late fifties and early sixties—the political aspect of this novel has come to seem less controversial, its liberal sentiments commanding general assent. When it first appeared in 1924, however, its satirical portrayal of the Raj had a polemical impact, which gave offense to (among others) the then vicereine of India[1]; and the novel was widely recognized as a telling attack on British imperialism. During the Second World War it was broadcast by the Germans, according to George Orwell, in a series of "shortened versions of books which they considered damaging to British prestige. . . . And so far as I know," he comments, "they didn't even have to resort to dishonest quotation. Just because the book was essentially truthful, it could be made to serve the purposes of Fascist propaganda."[2]

[1] E. M. Forster, *The Hill of Devi* (London: Edward Arnold and Co., 1953), p. 160.
[2] *The Collected Essays, Journalism and Letters of George Orwell,* ed. Sonia Orwell and Ian Angus (London: Secker and Warburg, 1968), IV, 35.

Twenty years after the publication of *A Passage to India*, Forster
was to write appreciatively of William Arnold's autobiographical
novel *Oakfield, or Fellowship in the East,* which had expressed (in
1853) the disillusion of a soldier turned imperial administrator—his
disgust at the quality of the average Britons whom he met in India, and
his questioning of their corporate achievement. "All the talk as to the
magnificent work of civilising Asia through British influence in India
is humbug," concludes the eponymous hero, "and it has grieved
many generous hearts before now to find it so." [3] A similar disillusion
is conveyed by Forster's novel—a skepticism about the value of imperial rule, a perception of its corrupting influence on both governors
and governed, and a distaste for the personal qualities and public
attitudes of Britons whom he had observed in India. The direct
political relevance of the novel might be slight, its constructive suggestions few, and its reformist impulse negligible, and for these
deficiencies it has been attacked by the politically conscious; yet its
challenge to complacent imperial assumptions was fundamental. Its
influence on educated élites, moreover, has been great, however difficult such matters are to quantify. Indeed the novel's literary excel-
lence, including the wicked precision (or apparent precision) of the
social comedy, and the sharpness of the satirical dissection of evil and
absurdity, make it potently persuasive; whereas the knowledge and
understanding of Edward Thompson's *An Indian Day* (1927) fail to
issue in fictional vitality, and George Orwell's denunciation of Empire
and imperialists in *Burmese Days* (1934) tends to be discredited by
its own stridency. *A Passage to India* was never intended primarily
as a political novel, but *as* a political novel it has had a notable
success.

So notable, indeed, that its documentary status may too often be
allowed to pass unchallenged, though it has been questioned from
time to time. Rose Macaulay, for example, argued that Forster was
attributing to Anglo-Indians of 1924 what were essentially prewar
patterns of behavior, and that sometimes "it looks as if Mr. Forster's
acutely vulnerable sense of humanity and his dislike of barbarous
nationalism and uncivil arrogance had over-reached itself, and made
him paint his natural enemies a shade too black." [4] And the authen-

---

[3] Quoted by E. M. Forster, *Two Cheers for Democracy* (London: Edward Arnold
and Co., 1951), p. 203.

[4] Rose Macaulay, *The Writings of E. M. Forster* (London: Hogarth Press, 1938),
p. 188. *The Times Literary Supplement,* on the other hand, reviewing the book
on 12 June 1924, remarked that "Not the least distinctive of Mr. E. M. Forster's

ticity of Forster's picture of race relations has been challenged more fundamentally by men with firsthand experience, including some who served in India for more years than Forster spent months in that country:

> You would suppose [writes "Philip Woodruff"] from a novel so brilliantly and delicately written as *A Passage to India*, that the English in India lived in a state of semi-hysteria, resolutely suppressing a fear that the Mutiny would come again. Perhaps it was so in Bengal, where three district magistrates of Midnapur were murdered in succession; it was not so in the North or in the South. In 1928, Charles Grant, District Magistrate of Saharanpur, was roused from the brief and hard-won sleep of a night in June by someone trying to undo his mosquito-net. He woke angrily to find a petitioner intent on explaining some trouble which for the moment Grant did not attempt to diagnose; he could not understand why the sentry who was supposed to keep watch on his house had let the man disturb him. Then he remembered that he had been kept awake one night by the sentry's boots and had banished him to the stables to guard the horses' corn—something far more in need of a guard than the District Magistrate. He turned to the petitioner who, it transpired, had lost his railway ticket and, being persecuted by inspectors, had escaped them and fled for succour to his father and mother.
>
> In camp, of course, a man slept unguarded in his tent; why should he not? He knew that in every village of his district he would be welcomed with grave courtesy. . . .[5]

Such reflections may seem to take us far from the novel itself, but the historical truth or falsity of Forster's picture can hardly be a matter of indifference to the critic, since a novel, however much a well-wrought urn or exquisitely planned half-acre tomb, is not autonomous in the sense of being independent of historical reality.

> The novel [as Professor Hough writes] because of its particularity in time and place . . . owes a considerable allegiance to social reporting and social history. It has not only to be a just representation of general nature, but also of specific facts and circumstances, in a way quite foreign to the other long narrative forms, epic and romance. The novel characteristically purports to represent the state of society at a particular

qualities is his fairness; his judgments are marked by an unfailing sincerity. The accurate blending of observation and insight is his outstanding virtue." (*Times Literary Supplement*, London, 1924, p. 370).

[5] Philip Woodruff (i.e. Philip Mason, C.I.E., O.B.E., Director of the Institute of Race Relations from 1958 to 1969, member of the Indian Civil Service from 1928 to 1947), *The Men Who Ruled India* (London: Jonathan Cape, 1953–54), II, 282.

time in a particular place; and part of its merit seems to be that it does
this justly. Dickens may mix up two poor laws and attack specific abuses
when they had really been superseded by others; but his London is
London in the early years of Queen Victoria's reign; and he is committed to getting the basic physical facts and social relations right.[6]

This is not to deny the novelist's right to select, shape, and interpret
his material, or the undeniable fact that novels may stand in a
variety of relations to historical reality. But it is to acknowledge
that there is a tension in the nature of the novel itself—the tension
between the author's right, which he shares with all artists, to present
his own vision of life, molding reality to a truth at once more personal
and more philosophical than history's, and on the other hand his
obligation (stronger in the novel than in any other genre) to hold
the mirror up to nature, showing things as they really are. This
tension cannot be eliminated: if a novelist commits himself entirely
to private vision, he will produce mere fantasy or propaganda; if he
commits himself entirely to rendering things as they are, he will
produce mere sociological reportage. The vitality of the novel as a
form depends on the maintenance of the tension between these opposing claims, and we must recognize the methodological problems
this gives rise to.

By the very nature of his discipline, the historian is likely to
retain a healthy skepticism about any novel's evidential value; but
the student of literature is continually tempted to construct his own
pseudo-history based on purely literary evidence—and evidence somewhat arbitrarily selected, on the assumption that the greater a work
of art is, the truer and more representative it must somehow be,
so that it can serve as the basis for wide cultural and historical gen-
eralizations. Forster's account of Anglo-India and of the Raj is the
only one encountered by most such undergraduates; yet it remains
one man's view, which—if we are seeking historical truth—must be
supplemented and corrected by other sources: by other fictional
works; by memoirs and eye-witness accounts, British and Indian; and
by historical assessments like Woodruff's own classic, *The Men Who
Ruled India*. The relevance of such historical "truth" to an evaluation of the novel itself is, of course, another question. If it is said—
as former I.C.S. officials tend to say—that this book gives a false
picture or an unrepresentative extreme, we may attempt to meet the

[6] Graham Hough, *An Essay on Criticism* (London: Duckworth and Co. Ltd.,
1966), p. 56.

criticism in two ways. Firstly, by amassing evidence about Anglo-Indian behavior in the period in question—either by random samples (such as are provided by Forster himself in *The Hill of Devi*) or by "Namierising" the whole Indian Civil Service—in an attempt to validate or invalidate the novel's testimony by external evidence. Or alternatively, we might seek to justify Forster's strategy in other terms: conceding that a balance sheet for British India would, historically considered, show far more in the credit column than Forster allows, we might argue, nonetheless, that he saw the imperial situation as poisoned at the core by assumptions of racial superiority, and that his novel is legitimately structured to reveal that central flaw. We might admit the charge of caricature, but employ it in Forster's defense, arguing that he may indeed distort observable reality but that like a caricaturist he distorts it to reveal essential truth. If we are then asked what is to prevent such a narrative from degenerating into propaganda, we must reply in terms of the writer's obligation to make his fictions appear probable, convincing. Whatever his own commitments, he must seem to be taking account of the complexity of human character and social circumstance; he must not deal in moral simplicities; he must give us the impression of being reasonably just in his procedures. We shall therefore invoke the criterion of "verisimilitude," however we define its relation to historical authenticity; so that more traditional approaches to the novel, stressing character creation (for example) rather than symbolism, will be wholly appropriate to evaluative as well as to descriptive criticism. It is, after all, the "life" of any novel that validates its "pattern."

III

Forster's critique of imperialism is based on ethical rather than political convictions. His novels, noted Cyril Connolly in 1938, "state the general conflict which is localised in the political conflict of today. His themes are the breaking down of barriers: between white and black, between class and class, between man and woman, between art and life. 'Only connect . . .' the motto of *Howards End,* might be the motto of all his work." [7] But that lesson is not presented primarily in terms of its political and economic application. Sharing,

---

[7] *Enemies of Promise* (London: George Routledge and Sons Ltd., 1938), p. 7.

Bloomsbury fashion, G. E. Moore's belief that "personal affections and aesthetic enjoyments include *all* the greatest, and *by far* the greatest, goods we can imagine," [8] Forster advocates a morality of private, not of public, life, though it has, of course, wider social implications. "I hate the idea of causes," he wrote in 1939, "and if I had to choose between betraying my country and betraying my friend, I hope I should have the guts to betray my country." [9] Whether the betrayal of his country (*anno domini* 1939) might involve the betrayal of not one but many friends, and the violation of personal affections and aesthetic enjoyments on a nightmare scale, he does not consider (any more than, in *The Hill of Devi*, he effectively balances the Maharajah's capacity for friendship against the injustice and suffering caused, presumably, by his maladministration). Personal relationships were for Forster a fundamental human value, axiomatically good, and from them he deduced the general need for tolerance, good temper, and sympathy. However ineffectual these virtues might be in a confrontation with Nazi Germany (of whose vileness he was well aware), "they are," he insisted, "what matter really, and if the human race is not to collapse they must come to the front before long." [10] Their admitted inadequacy in face of force and violence did not sap his conviction that they are good, and force and violence evil—that civilization can indeed be defined as those intervals in history when force and violence have not prevailed—intervals in which, says Forster, "all the great creative actions [and] all the decent human relations" tend to occur.[11]

Such assumptions underlie Forster's distaste for British rule in India; not just because it rested ultimately on force, but also because the British ruling caste there seemed to him to lack the human qualities he valued most. In his "Notes on the English Character" (1920) he had deplored the middle-class public-school ideal and its consequences, which he saw as the stunting of personality and the instillation of prejudice. The products of this system, he wrote,

> go forth into a world that is not entirely composed of public-school men or even of Anglo-Saxons, but of men who are as various as the sands of the sea; into a world of whose richness and subtlety they have no conception. They go forth into it with well-developed bodies, fairly

[8] G. E. Moore, *Principia Ethica* (1903), quoted by J. K. Johnstone, *The Bloomsbury Group* (London: Secker and Warburg, 1954), p. 24.
[9] *Two Cheers for Democracy*, p. 78.
[10] *Ibid.*, p. 77.
[11] *Ibid.*, pp. 80–81.

developed minds, and undeveloped hearts. And it is this undeveloped heart that is largely responsible for the difficulties of Englishmen abroad.[12]

The defects which he observed in the British in India were attributable, however, not merely to their national character and upbringing but to their political role there. Believing (like Adela Quested) in "the sanctity of personal relationships,"[13] Forster was appalled by the corruption of personal relationships produced by imperial rule, with its harsh divisions of humanity into governors and governed, white and colored, and its hierarchical structuring of both racial and social relationships. The narrative begins and ends with discussions less of liberty than of equality and fraternity—of the possibility of genuine friendship between Briton and Indian; and the moral-political challenge is no less effective for this personalized basis. Rudeness, unkindness, insensitivity of the kind shown by Mesdames Callendar and Lesley, by Mrs. Turton, or by Ronny Heaslop, are themselves an indictment of the system which permits (or still worse, encourages) them. "The decent Anglo-Indian of today," Forster wrote in 1922, "realises that the great blunder of the past is neither political nor economic nor educational, but social; that he was associated with a system that supported rudeness . . . , and is paying the penalty. . . . Never in history did ill-breeding contribute so much towards the dissolution of an Empire."[14]

The gulf between rulers and ruled, between white and colored, is, however, only the most obvious of the divisions between man and man presented in this novel. In the opening description of Chandrapore, the three levels of the city, each inhabited by a different racial group, presents a social stratification which might be thought peculiar to the imperial situation; but the narrative soon forces us to realize that there are many more divisions in India than Empire can be held responsible for. There are the divisions of class and wealth, for example, and still more of religion and of caste, which seem essential, inevitable features of the Indian scene (so that when Aziz mounts his multi-racial, multi-religious picnic, "trouble after trouble encountered him, because [we are told] he had challenged the spirit of the Indian

[12] *Abinger Harvest,* Pocket ed. (London: Edward Arnold, 1961), p. 13.
[13] *A Passage to India,* Everyman Ed. (London: J. M. Dent and Sons Ltd., 1948), p. 69.
[14] Article in *Nation and Athenaeum,* January 1922. Quoted by Macaulay, *op. cit.,* pp. 189–90.

earth, which tries to keep men in compartments").[15] Reluctantly, regretfully, but honestly, the novel presents the separateness of man from man, the divisive forces at work in humanity, and their concomitants of embarrassment, awkwardness, cruelty, pain, contempt, indifference, and hatred.

To withstand such forces is the supreme test of the Forsterian ethic. His liberal, humane ideal seems exemplified in Fielding, who believed not that the shibboleths of the Club embodied wisdom, but that "the world . . . is a globe of men who are trying to reach one another and can best do so by the help of goodwill plus culture and intelligence. . . ." [16] The formula of goodwill plus culture and intelligence is admirable, and the novel shows impressively how much it can achieve in terms of friendship established, misunderstandings overcome, and prejudices defied; especially when to these Schlegelian values from *Howards End* is added a kind of masculine toughness, which enables Fielding to stand out against the pressures of his tribe. He is clearly a member of the true aristocracy in which Forster believed—"not an aristocracy of power, based upon rank and influence, but an aristocracy of the sensitive, the considerate and the plucky." [17] There can be no doubt of the admiration which the author feels for him; and yet, as the novel progresses, we are made to doubt whether his values are wholly adequate—whether "goodwill plus culture and intelligence" are enough to cope with the problems and mysteries of life. As Fielding leaves the Club after the dreadful scene in which he defies the Collector, declaring his belief in his friend's innocence, he pauses on the verandah to contemplate the Marabar Hills in the distance:

> It was the last moment of the light, and as he gazed at the Marabar Hills they seemed to move graciously towards him like a queen, and their charm became the sky's. At the moment they vanished they were everywhere, the cool benediction of the night descended, the stars sparkled, and the whole universe was a hill. Lovely, exquisite moment— but passing the Englishman with averted face and on swift wings. He experienced nothing himself; it was as if someone had told him there was such a moment, and he was obliged to believe. And he felt dubious and discontented suddenly, and wondered whether he was really and truly successful as a human being. After forty years' experience he had learnt to manage his life and make the best of it on advanced European

[15] *A Passage to India*, p. 109.
[16] *Ibid.*, p. 50.
[17] *Two Cheers for Democracy*, p. 82.

lines, had developed his personality, explored his limitations, controlled his passions—and he had done it all without becoming either pedantic or worldly. A creditable achievement; but as the moment passed he felt he ought to have been working at something else the whole time—he didn't know at what, never would know, never could know, and that was why he felt sad.[18]

No irony inheres in the phrase "a creditable achievement," for the validity of the claim has been established fully by the narrative itself; yet even now at Fielding's finest hour, Forster suggests some radical limitation in him. What he misses, as he gazes at the Marabar Hills, is something more than an aesthetic experience: it seems to partake of the religious, and to suggest a spiritual dimension lacking in his own life and Miss Quested's. When, much later, these two are discussing the Marabar Caves incident, we are told that she, unable to explain it, "was at the end of her spiritual tether, and so was he. Were there worlds beyond which they could never touch, or did all that is possible enter their consciousness? They could not tell. . . . Perhaps life is a mystery, not a muddle; they could not tell. Perhaps the hundred Indias which fuss and squabble so tiresomely are one, and the universe they mirror is one. They had not the apparatus for judging." [19] "Their creator," observes Lord David Cecil, "does not seem to have the apparatus either";[20] and the metaphysical uncertainties of this novel have preoccupied many critics. Clearly, Forster presents Fielding's liberal-agnostic-humanitarian philosophy as a good one—and the novel demonstrates its potency for good in human relationships; but equally clearly Forster seems to suggest that there are dimensions of experience, problems (or mysteries) of evil and negation, symbolized by the Marabar Hills with their extraordinary caves, which demand an essentially religious explanation, however little confidence he has in his own ability to provide one.

IV

Forster's politics depend on ethics—on a moral vision partial, admittedly, yet penetrating and disturbing. And his ethics depend, in this work at any rate, on metaphysics, though these are a matter for imaginative exploration rather than dogmatic commitment. To

[18] *A Passage to India*, p. 165.
[19] *Ibid.*, p. 229.
[20] *Poets and Story-Tellers* (London: Constable, 1949), p. 186.

systematize too neatly is to risk falsifying the novel's spiritual insights: we may often hesitate between an overtly theological and a more elusively symbolic reading; and we shall do well to accept some uncertainties, mysteries, and doubts without too irritable a reaching after fact and reason. Yet the major emphases are plain enough. Many critics—Montgomery Belgion, for example[21]—have noted in Forster's writings an animus against Christianity and its exponents. This is hardly the point of his irony at the expense of the official religion of Anglo-India, but it is very relevant to his dismissal of the missionary Miss Quested meets on her homeward voyage, and also to his treatment of "old Mr. Graysford and young Mr. Sorley." [22] These two worthy men are immortalized in ridicule, like flies in amber, by a single paragraph. For them the kingdom of God is not of this world; but revolutionaries and reformers have always wanted to build the City of God on earth, and Forster yearns for human brotherhood now, not in a hypothetical hereafter. (His own novel ends with a postponement, but a more reluctant one.) And furthermore, Forster sees in the missionaries' teaching, as in Islam, a principle of exclusiveness, in contrast to the Hindu plea for an all-inclusive love embracing the whole of creation. The famous rejection of the wasps implies a comparison with the British excluding Indians from the Club, and (however comic the mode) it thus tends, fairly or unfairly, to discredit the missionaries' brand of religion.

Mrs. Moore's Christianity compels more admiration, for she brings its ethical imperatives to bear directly on the facts of Empire. "The English *are* out here to be pleasant," she tells Ronny. ". . . Because India is part of the earth. And God has put us on the earth in order to be pleasant to each other. God . . . is . . . love." [23] Her own gift for personal relationships, based on intuitive wisdom rather than on dogma, supports this profession of faith; and her acceptance of the wasp ("Pretty dear") associates her with the Hinduism Forster obviously admires, not with the missionaries. And yet, at the Marabar, she fails; and with her failure the validity of her Christianity itself is called in question.

The disastrous climax to the Marabar outing can be accounted for to some extent in straightforward psychological terms: an old lady whose health is failing has a physical-emotional collapse; a young

[21] Montgomery Belgion, "The Diabolism of Mr. E. M. Forster," *The Criterion*, XIV (1934–35), 54–73.

[22] *A Passage to India*, p. 28.

[23] *Ibid.*, p. 40.

woman, who has been undergoing great nervous strain, breaks down and has a hallucination of attempted rape. But beyond this, we have the impression of the caves as being (as it were) spiritual sounding boards, reflecting back or "echoing" in an intensified, distorted form what characters bring to them. Mrs. Moore had had God constantly in her thoughts since she entered India, but "oddly enough, he satisfied her less. She needs must pronounce his name frequently, as the greatest she knew, yet she had never found it less efficacious." [24] She had had doubts, too, about whether too much fuss is not made about marriage and personal relationships. And now these lurking doubts are intensified, multiplied, and exaggerated in a nightmarish echo as they are reflected back to her soul by the Marabar Caves:

> . . . the echo began in some indescribable way to undermine her hold on life. Coming at a moment when she chanced to be fatigued, it had managed to murmur: "Pathos, piety, courage—they exist, but are identical, and so is filth. Everything exists, nothing has value." If one had spoken vileness in that place, or quoted lofty poetry, the comment would have been the same—"ou-boum." . . . [And] suddenly, at the edge of her mind, religion appeared, poor little talkative Christianity, and she knew that all its divine words from "Let there be Light" to "It is finished" only amounted to "boum." Then she was terrified over an area larger than usual; . . . the mood of her last two months took definite form at last, and she realized that she didn't want to write to her children, didn't want to communicate with any one, not even with God.[25]

This is presented not as insight but as spiritual failure on Mrs. Moore's part, and (together with her illness) it accounts for her rapid decline in moral stature as she becomes selfish, self-regarding, and cynical. ("Her Christian tenderness had gone, or had developed into a hardness, a just irritation against the human race." [26]) She remains capable of flashes of spiritual insight, as when she proclaims her faith in Aziz' innocence; her spirit is mysteriously associated with Adela's recantation, and his acquittal; and her influence, to quote Forster himself, reappears in the third section of the novel;[27] but she never regains the status which she had for us earlier in the story, and we

[24] *Ibid.*, p. 41.

[25] *Ibid.*, pp. 128–29. That this passage is quoted in virtually every critique of the novel is an indication of its centrality.

[26] *Ibid.*, p. 172.

[27] Angus Wilson, "A Conversation with E. M. Forster," *Encounter*, Vol. IX, No. 5 (November 1957), 54.

are left to speculate whether her collapse is indeed merely personal or whether it implies for Forster basic inadequacies in the Christianity on which she had relied. (We may also find ourselves questioning, more fundamentally, the adequacy of his own conception of the Christianity which he rejects.)

The most ambitious gloss which Forster offers on these mysteries of evil and negation is provided by Professor Godbole in the course of his comments on the Marabar episode: "Good and evil are different, as their names imply. But, in my humble opinion, they are both of them aspects of my Lord. He is present in the one, absent in the other, and the difference between presence and absence is great, as great as my feeble mind can grasp. Yet absence implies presence, absence is not non-existence, and we are therefore entitled to repeat, 'Come, come, come, come.' " [28] Rhetorically and thematically this is linked with other passages like Godbole's song to Krishna (in which the god neglects to come), or the description of the landscape on the way to Marabar, in which "in vain did each item . . . call out: 'Come, come.' There was not enough god to go round." [29] The cumulative effect is to establish the Marabar Caves as an evil place— not of course in a primitively magical sense, but symbolically, as representing an extreme of human experience, a spiritual vacuum which can be expressed theologically as an absence of god, morally as an absence of love.

The idea is taken up and reorchestrated in the final "Temple" section of the novel. The Hindu festival is muddled, chaotic, "a frustration of . . . reason and form"; but amid the confusion god is born, symbolically, and love celebrated. The singers "loved all men, the whole universe, and scraps of their past, tiny splinters of detail, emerged for a moment to melt into the universal warmth. Thus Godbole . . . remembered an old woman he had met in Chandrapore days. Chance brought her into his mind . . . and he impelled her by his spiritual force to that place where completeness can be found. . . . [He] remembered a wasp seen he forgot where, perhaps on a stone. He loved the wasp equally, he impelled it likewise, he was imitating God. . . ." [30] The love Godbole celebrates is all-inclusive, as we see when his reiterated prayer to Krishna is answered, when the God no longer neglects to come: "Infinite Love took upon itself the shape of SHRI-KRISHNA, and saved the world. All sorrow was annihilated, not

[28] *A Passage to India*, p. 154.
[29] *Ibid.*, p. 73.
[30] *Ibid.*, pp. 249–50.

only for Indians, but for foreigners, birds, caves, railways, and the stars; all became joy, all laughter; there had never been disease nor doubt, misunderstanding, cruelty, fear." [31] The consequences in human terms are the inclusion of all ranks, all classes, all castes (even the Sweepers) in this ceremony; the muting of conflict between rival claimants to the throne; the purging of Mau "from suspicion and self-seeking"; and the ending of the estrangement between Aziz and Fielding. Yet this paradisal moment is soon over; all the familiar conflicts re-emerge; and the novel ends as it began with the separation of man from man, and the impossibility of true friendship and communion. Hence most readers have been left to speculate with some bewilderment on the precise import of Forster's symbolism, the nature of his implied theology, and his degree of commitment to what he renders here in terms of Hinduism (a question complicated by his very different account of the Festival of Gokul Ashtami in *The Hill of Devi*).

V

A Passage to India was the last of Forster's novels (in spite of a few subsequent false starts);[32] and it presents the fullest articulation of his ethical and "religious" intuitions, which are adumbrated in varying degrees in earlier novels and in his short stories. Much critical discussion has therefore concerned itself with the nature and validity of these insights; but the novel is also his aesthetic masterpiece, the most closely textured, highly wrought, and carefully structured of all his writings; and its artistry has been another major focus of attention.

Can "pattern," Forster himself asks in *Aspects of the Novel*, "be combined with the immense richness of material which life provides? Wells and James would agree that it cannot. Wells would go on to say that life should be given the preference, and must not be whittled or distended for a pattern's sake. My own prejudices are with Wells." [33] The declaration is important, but it would be misleading as an indication of his own creative practice. He recognized that pattern in a novel "appeals to our aesthetic sense, . . . causes us to see the book as a whole"; and that although we may not apprehend it

---

[31] *Ibid.*, p. 251.
[32] Wilson, *op. cit.*, p. 55.
[33] *Aspects of the Novel* (New York: Harcourt, Brace and World, Inc., 1927), p. 233.

visually, "we . . . have a pleasure without knowing why"—a pleasure
which may then be analyzed in terms of geometrical or other similes.[34]
"Beauty is sometimes the *shape* of the book," [35] he maintains; and
although he did not "pre-figure a shape" for his own novels,[36] he seems
to have found visual analogies helpful in his evolution of their form.
Thus he can say of the festival description in *A Passage to India* that
"it was architecturally necessary. I needed a lump, or a Hindu temple
if you like—a mountain standing up." [37] Painting provided the con-
cept of "pattern" in artistic composition; but elsewhere, in his discussion of "rhythm," for example, he found musical analogies more
helpful, maintaining indeed that "music, though it does not employ
human beings, though it is governed by intricate laws, nevertheless
does offer in its final expression a type of beauty which fiction might
achieve in its own way." [38] Both sets of analogies point to his preoccupation with the aesthetic aspects of form; and the tripartite structuring of *A Passage to India,* the elaborate cross-references in plot, symbolism, and phraseology, the pervasive yet subtle use of rhythm in
his "easy" sense of "repetition plus variation," [39] all show his awareness of the novel as literary artifact. Yet his generous indignation,
his sympathetic insights, his sensitive vivid rendering of scenery, social
relationships and a wide range of individual characters, all demon-
strate his commitment to reality—though a reality more finely conceived than anything in Wells's fiction. *A Passage to India* is his most
triumphant reconciliation of the claims of "pattern" and of "life."
He achieves in it the harmonious internal order which can be found
(he believed) only in art;[40] but his art is designed to illuminate and
influence life as well as to delight aesthetically. A work of art, he
argues, is "infectious"—it has "the power of transforming the person
who encounters it towards the condition of the person who created
it";[41] but he is no simple moralist, for in his view the sustaining power
of art is not a matter of direct moral reinforcement: in 1934 he
quoted some lines by Davenant "not because they are great poetry
. . . but because they have happened to deposit a grain of strength

[34] *Ibid.,* p. 215.
[35] *Ibid.,* p. 218 (my italics).
[36] *Writers at Work: The "Paris Review" Interviews,* ed. Malcolm Cowley (London:
Secker and Warburg, 1958), p. 29.
[37] *Ibid.,* p. 27.
[38] *Aspects of the Novel,* p. 241.
[39] *Ibid.,* p. 240.
[40] *Two Cheers for Democracy,* p. 101.
[41] *Ibid.,* p. 125.

in my mind. They are so lovely in their little way, and they have helped towards that general belief in loveliness which is part of our outfit against brutality." [42] Yet he is obviously no mere aesthete either, the great novel being for him a thing of beauty *and* of truth. Thus rhythm—to take only one aspect of his fictional technique—has a dual function in *A Passage to India*: as well as helping to achieve formal unity, and delighting us by "its lovely waxing and waning" which "[fills] us with surprise and freshness and hope," [43] it also helps to establish the structure of symbolic meaning in the novel, and thus serves to mediate the author's moral and religious vision.

Virginia Woolf, dividing novelists into preachers and teachers on the one hand, and pure artists on the other, recognized that Forster "has a strong impulse to belong to both camps at once. He has many of the instincts and aptitudes of the pure artist . . . —an exquisite prose style, an acute sense of comedy, a power of creating characters in a few strokes which live in an atmosphere of their own; but he is at the same time highly conscious of a message. Behind the rainbow of wit and sensibility there is a vision which he is determined that we shall see." [44] The reconciliation of such opposites she saw as one of his main problems as an artist. "Here," she observed, ". . . is a difficult family of gifts to persuade to live in harmony together: satire and sympathy; fantasy and fact; poetry and a prim moral sense"; to which, later in her essay, she adds "realism and mysticism." [45] These potentially conflicting elements derive from different modes of vision, and result in a variety of technical problems. The success with which these have been solved in *A Passage to India* is a matter of continuing debate, in which technical analysis cannot usefully be distinguished from interpretative comment. But the kind of solution to which Forster himself aspired may well be indicated by his praise of Ibsen's blend of realism and symbolism:

[A] connection is found [he wrote in 1928] between objects that lead different types of existence; they reinforce one another and each lives more intensely than before. Consequently his stage throbs with a mysteriousness for which no obvious preparation has been made, with beckonings, tremblings, sudden compressions of the air, and his characters as they wrangle among the oval tables and stoves are watched by an unseen

[42] *Abinger Harvest*, p. 89.
[43] *Aspects of the Novel*, p. 239.
[44] *The Death of the Moth and Other Essays* (London: The Hogarth Press, 1942), p. 107.
[45] *Ibid.*, pp. 106, 108.

power which slips between their words. . . . The symbolism never
holds up the action, because it is part of the action, and because Ibsen
was a poet, to whom creation and craftsmanship were one. . . . Everything rings true and echoes far because it is in the exact place which
its surroundings require.[46]

Forster himself, like every great novelist, was both craftsman and
creator. He has warned us that much of what seems technical clever-
ness was not consciously contrived;[47] and his writing of a novel was
itself a process of discovery. All the major steps in the plot were not
present in the original conception; but, he told interviewers for the
Paris Review, "there must be something, some major object towards
which one is to approach. When I began *A Passage to India* I knew
that something important happened in the Malabar [*sic*] Caves, and
that it would have a central place in the novel—but I didn't know
what it would be. . . . The Malabar Caves represented an area in
which concentration can take place. A cavity. . . . They were something to focus everything up: they were to engender an event like an
egg." [48] This is surprising, in view of the assurance with which the
leit-motif of the Marabar is sounded in the first and last sentences of
the opening chapter; but it serves to emphasize the exploratory,
heuristic nature of great art for the author as well as his readers,
while Oliver Stallybrass's account of Forster's manuscripts shows on
the other hand how much careful revision, how much conscious
craftsmanship, lies behind the finally achieved perfection.

If the high estimate suggested by that phrase cannot command
unanimous assent, each critic must offer his own limiting judgments;
but we should do so with proper humility, remembering that the
novel will be read when our reservations are forgotten; remembering
too—whether or not we accept it—Forster's own caveat on criticism
as "the sensitive dissection of particular works of art":

> What did the artist hope to do? [he asks] What means did he employ,
> subconscious or conscious? Did he succeed, and if his success was partial
> where did he fail? In such a dissection the tools should break as soon as
> they encounter any living tissue. The apparatus is nothing, the specimen
> all.[49]

[46] *Abinger Harvest,* pp. 102-3.
[47] *Writers at Work,* p. 32.
[48] *Ibid.,* pp. 26–27. Cf. Wilson, *op. cit.,* p. 56: "E.M.F. 'I have very few notes
[i.e. when writing]. The plot is in my mind. Then I alter as I go on from day to
day. The re-writing is done in "blocks".' "
[49] *Two Cheers for Democracy,* p. 119.

A Passage to India

by Lionel Trilling

In 1910, following the publication of *Howards End*, Forster projected two novels but wrote neither. The next year he finished a play,
The Heart of Bosnia, which, by his own account, was not good, and
which has never been produced or published. In 1912, Forster, in
company with [Goldsworthy Lowes] Dickinson and R. C. Trevelyan,
sailed for India. Dickinson, travelling on one of the fellowships established by Albert Kahn in the interests of international understanding, had official visits and tours to make and the friends separated
at Bombay. But their itineraries crossed several times and they spent
a fortnight as guests of the Maharajah of Chhatarpur who loved
Dickinson and philosophy—" 'Tell me, Mr. Dickinson, where is
God?' " the Maharajah said. " 'Can Herbert Spencer lead me to him,
or should I prefer George Henry Lewes? Oh when will Krishna come
and be my friend? Oh Mr. Dickinson!' "

The two travellers came away from India with widely different
feelings. Dickinson, who was to love China, was not comfortable in
India. Displeased as he was by her British rulers, he was not pleased
with India itself. "There is no solution to the problem of governing
India," he wrote. "Our presence is a curse both to them and to us.
Our going away will be worse. I believe that to the last word. And
why can't the races meet? Simply because the Indians *bore* the English.
That is the simple adamantine fact." It is not an enlightening or
even a serious view of the situation, and Forster, dissenting from it,
speaks of the "peace and happiness" which he himself found in India
in 1912 and again on his second visit ten years later.

"A Passage to India." *From E. M. Forster by Lionel Trilling (New York: New
Directions, 1943; London: Hogarth Press Limited, 1944), pp. 117–38. Copyright
1943 by New Directions Publishing Corporation. Reprinted by permission of New
Directions Publishing Corporation and Laurence Pollinger Limited. This essay is
reprinted complete except for two introductory paragraphs referring back to*
Howards End, *and a summary of the plot of the novel.*

The best fruit of the Indian journey was to be *A Passage to India*, but meanwhile Forster wrote several short pieces on Indian life of which two, "The Suppliant" and "Advance, India!" (both reprinted in *Abinger Harvest*) admirably depict the comic, sad confusion of a nation torn between two cultures.

He began to sketch the Indian novel, but the war postponed its completion for a decade. And the war quite destroyed the project for a critical study of Samuel Butler, with whose mind Forster's has community at so many points. But the war, which sent Forster to non-combatant service in Egypt, developed in him the interests in Imperial conduct and policy which the Indian tour had begun. Hitherto Forster's political concern had been intense but perhaps abstract; now it became increasingly immediate. The three Egyptian years gave him not only the material for two books and many essays, but also a firm position on the Imperial question.

The first of Forster's Egyptian books is the guidebook, *Alexandria*; its introductory account of the city's history gives Forster the opportunity to display his love of the Hellenic and naturalistic, his contempt for the Christian and theological; its second part arranges tours to points of interest, and the whole job is scholarly, attractive and efficient.[1] Much less can be said for *Pharos and Pharillon,* another venture into Alexandrian history and local colour. The volume is infused with the archness which has been noted earlier as the fault of Forster's first historical essays; the years have but intensified it. Under Forster's implacable gentleness, the past becomes what it should never be, quaint, harmless and ridiculous. Menelaos, Alexander, the Ptolemies, the Jews, the Arabs, the Christian theologians, the very lighthouse itself, all become submerged in high irony. This desperately persistent fault of taste is all the more surprising because Forster has himself so rightly characterized it in one of his best essays, "The Consolations of History."

> It is pleasant to be transferred from an office where one is afraid of a sergeant-major into an office where one can intimidate generals, and perhaps that is why History is so attractive to the more timid among us. We can recover self-confidence by snubbing the dead. . . . Tight

[1] The historical part of the book is a model of popularization without condescension. Especially notable are the lucid pages on the Alexandrian mystics; the exposition of Plotinus has the quality of creative insight into mystical thought that makes *A Passage to India* so remarkable. It is worth noting that Dickinson in his youth was an enthusiastic student of Plotinus.

little faces from Oxford, fish-shaped faces from Cambridge,—we cannot
help having our dreams.

The same fault of lofty whimsicality inheres in other of the sketches
which in *Abinger Harvest* are collected under the rubric of "The
Past." Sufficiently objectionable in "Captain Edward Gibbon" and in
"Voltaire's Laboratory," it becomes really bad in "Trooper Silas
Tompkyns Comberbacke" and in "The Abbeys' Difficulties," the first
of which dramatically reveals the open secret that the Trooper's real
name was Samuel Taylor Coleridge, the second that the young people with whom the Abbeys had difficulty were Fanny and John Keats.
A single sentence of *Pharos and Pharillon* points away from this
slim, feasting antiquarianism; speaking of Fort Kait Bey, Forster
mentions the holes in it "made by Admiral Seymour when he bom-
barded the Fort in 1882 and laid the basis of our intercourse with
modern Egypt." In 1920 Forster wrote his note for *The Government
of Egypt,* a pamphlet of the International Section of the Labour Research Department, a Fabian organization.[2] Although it does little
save support the Committee's recommendation that Egypt be given
either dominion status or autonomy and although it is scarcely interesting in itself, it indicates Forster's increasing interest in public
affairs.
It was an angry interest. In 1934 Forster was to publish his biography of Dickinson, who had died two years before. Perhaps because
Dickinson's life lacked tension or tone, perhaps because Forster wrote
under some reserve, the biography is not a work of high distinction,
but it serves to suggest the political atmosphere in which Forster
lived. The crown of Dickinson's political life was his fight against
what he called International Anarchy; his weapon, soon taken from
his hands, was the League of Nations. He hoped to raise the minds of
men above "the fighting attitude" of practical politics, but he could
never, he confessed, formulate clearly "the great problem of the relation of ideals to passion and interest." This is, of course, Forster's
own insistent question, but Forster's is an angrier mind than Dickinson's and any uncertainty he feels about the ultimate problems of
politics does not prevent him from speaking out on matters of the moment.
England after the war was tense with class antagonism. In 1920

[2] The 1921 edition of the pamphlet bears the imprint, "The Fabian Research
Department."

Forster became for a year the literary editor of the *Daily Herald,* a Labour paper to whose weekly literary page many well-known writers of liberal leanings contributed reviews. In the following years the amount of Forster's literary and political journalism, collected and uncollected, was considerable.

The political pieces are suffused with disillusionment about the war, a foreboding that a new war is imminent, a hatred of the stupidities of class rule. They pretend neither to originality of sentiment nor to practical perspicacity; they express, sometimes with anger, sometimes with bitterness, sometimes only with a kind of salutary irritation and disgust, the old emotions—the 19th century emotions, we almost feel, and we salute their directness—of a rational democrat confronting foolishness and pretence. Perhaps the most successful of these pieces is the essay "Me, Them and You." It is a review of the Sargent exhibition of 1925 in which, among all the aristocratic portraits, Sargent's pleasant, fanciful war picture, "Gassed," was hung. The situation was made for the satirist and Forster takes advantage of it in one of the truly successful pieces of modern invective.

> The portraits dominated. Gazing at each other over our heads, they said, "What would the country do without us? We have got the decorations and the pearls, we make fashions and wars, we have the largest houses and eat the best food, and control the most important industries, and breed the most valuable children, and ours is the Kingdom and the Power and the Glory." And, listening to their chorus, I felt this was so, and my clothes fitted worse and worse, and there seemed in all the universe no gulf wider than the gulf between Them and Me—no wider gulf, until I encountered You.
>
> You had been plentiful enough in the snow outside (your proper place) but I had not expected to find You here in the place of honour, too. Yours was by far the largest picture in the show. You were hung between Lady Cowdray and the Hon. Mrs. Langman, and You were entitled "Gassed." You were of godlike beauty—for the upper classes only allow the lower classes to appear in art on condition that they wash themselves and have classical features. These conditions you fulfilled. A line of golden-haired Apollos moved along a duck-board from left to right with bandages over their eyes. They had been blinded by mustard gas. Others sat peacefully in the foreground, others approached through the middle distance. The battlefield was sad but tidy. No one complained, no one looked lousy or overtired, and the aeroplanes overhead struck the necessary note of the majesty of England. It was all that a great war picture should be, and it was modern because it managed to tell a new sort of lie. Many ladies and gentlemen fear that Romance is

passing out of war with the sabres and the chargers. Sargent's master-piece reassures them. He shows them that it is possible to suffer with a quiet grace under the new conditions, and Lady Cowdray and the Hon. Mrs. Langman, as they looked over the twenty feet of canvas that divided them, were able to say, "How touching," instead of "How obscene."

Less remarkable but filled with a fine irritation is the piece on the British Empire Exhibition at Wembley ("An Empire Is Born") and another on the Queen's Doll House ("The Doll Souse"). Forster's old antipathy to the clergy turns up again in political form in the verses which answer Bishop Welldon's public complaint of the profanity of the Labour Members of Parliament. One of the best of his essays, "My Wood," describes the growth of the property sense in himself after the purchase of a new tract of wood—"The other day I heard a twig snap in [my wood]. I was annoyed at first, for I thought that some-one was blackberrying, and depreciating the value of the undergrowth. On coming nearer, I saw it was not a man who had trodden on the twig and snapped it, but a bird, and I felt pleased. My bird." The essay is especially to be noted because it states with almost startling explicitness a view of life which has been implicit in the novels:

> Our life on earth is, and ought to be, material and carnal. But we have not yet learned to manage our materialism and carnality properly; they are still entangled with the desire for ownership; where (in the words of Dante) "Possession is one with loss."

Over the anomalies of literary censorship Forster had long been exercised.[3] In 1939 he was appointed by the Lord Chancellor to the Committee to examine the Law of Defamatory Libel. His 1935 ad-dress to the Paris *Congrès International des Ecrivains* on the subject of literary freedom constitutes a declaration of political faith.

> It seems to me that if nations keep on amassing armaments, they can no more help discharging their filth than an animal which keeps on eating can stop itself from excreting. This being so, my job and the job of those who feel with me is an interim job. We have just to go on tinkering as well as we can with our old tools until the crash comes. When the crash comes, nothing is any good. After it—if there is an after—the task of civilization will be carried on by people whose train-ing has been different from my own.

[3] He deals with censorship in "Mrs. Grundy at the Parkers'" (*Abinger Harvest*) and in his introduction to Alec Craig's *The Banned Books of England* (1937).

I am worried by thoughts of a war oftener than by thoughts of my own death, yet the line to be adopted over both these nuisances is the same. One must behave as if one is immortal, and as if civilization is eternal. Both statements are false—I shall not survive, no more will the great globe itself—both of them must be assumed to be true if we are to go on eating and working and travelling, and keep open a few breathing holes for the human spirit.

In 1922 Forster made a second journey to India and took up again the Indian story he had projected. *A Passage to India* appeared with great success in 1924.

A Passage to India is Forster's best known and most widely read novel. Public and political reasons no doubt account for this; in England the book was a matter for controversy and its success in America, as Forster himself explains it, was due to the superiority Americans could feel at the English botch of India. But the public, political nature of the book is not extraneous; it inheres in the novel's very shape and texture.

By many standards of criticism, this public, political quality works for good. *A Passage to India* is the most comfortable and even the most conventional of Forster's novels. It is under the control not only of the author's insight; a huge, hulking physical fact which he is not alone in seeing, requiring that the author submit to its veto-power. Consequently, this is the least surprising of Forster's novels, the least capricious and, indeed, the least personal. It quickly establishes the pattern for our emotions and keeps to it. We are at once taught to withhold our sympathies from the English officials, to give them to Mrs. Moore and to the "renegade" Fielding, to regard Adela Quested with remote interest and Aziz and his Indian friends with affectionate understanding.

Within this pattern we have, to be sure, all the quick, subtle modifications, the sudden strictness or relentings of judgment which are the best stuff of Forster's social imagination. But always the pattern remains public, simple and entirely easy to grasp. What distinguishes it from the patterns of similarly public and political novels is the rigor of its objectivity; it deals with unjust, hysterical emotion and it leads us, not to intense emotions about justice, but to cool poise and judgment—if we do not relent in our contempt for Ronny, we are at least forced to be aware that he is capable of noble, if stupid, feelings; the English girl who has the hallucination of an attempted rape by a native has engaged our sympathy by her rather dull decency; we are permitted no easy response to the benign Mrs. Moore, or to

Fielding, who stands out against his own people, or to the native physician who is wrongly accused. This restraint of our emotions is an important element in the book's greatness.

With the public nature of the story goes a chastened and somewhat more public style than is usual with Forster, and a less arbitrary manner. Forster does not abandon his right to intrude into the novel, but his manner of intrusion is more circumspect than ever before. Perhaps this is because here, far less than in the English and Italian stories, he is in possession of truth; the Indian gods are not his gods, they are not genial and comprehensible. So far as the old Mediterranean deities of wise impulse and loving intelligence can go in India, Forster is at home; he thinks they can go far but not all the way, and a certain retraction of the intimacy of his style reflects his uncertainty. The acts of imagination by which Forster conveys the sense of the Indian gods are truly wonderful; they are, nevertheless, the acts of imagination not of a master of the truth but of an intelligent neophyte, still baffled.

So the public nature of the novel cannot be said to work wholly for good. For the first time Forster has put himself to the test of verisimilitude. Is this the truth about India? Is this the way the English act?—always? sometimes? never? Are Indians like this?—all of them? some of them? Why so many Moslems and so few Hindus? Why so much Hindu religion and so little Moslem? And then, finally, the disintegrating question, What is to be done?

Forster's gallery of English officials has of course been disputed in England; there have been many to say that the English are not like that. Even without knowledge we must suppose that the Indian Civil Service has its quota of decent, devoted and humble officials. But if Forster's portraits are perhaps angry exaggerations, anger can be illuminating—the English of Forster's Chandrapore are the limits toward which the English in India must approach, for Lord Acton was right, power does corrupt, absolute power does corrupt absolutely.

As for the representation of the Indians, that too can be judged here only on *a priori* grounds. Although the Indians are conceived in sympathy and affection, they are conceived with these emotions alone, and although all of them have charm, none of them has dignity; they touch our hearts but they never impress us. Once, at his vindication feast, Aziz is represented as "full of civilization . . . complete, dignified, rather hard" and for the first time Fielding treats him "with diffidence," but this only serves to remind us how lacking in dignity Aziz usually is. Very possibly this is the effect that Indians make upon even sensitive Westerners; Dickinson, as we have seen, was bored by them, and generations of subjection can diminish the habit of dignity and teach grown men the strategy of the little child.

These are not matters that we can settle; that they should have arisen at all is no doubt a fault of the novel. Quite apart from the fact that questions of verisimilitude diminish illusion, they indicate a certain inadequacy in the conception of the story. To represent the official English as so unremittingly bad and the Indians as so unremittingly feeble is to prevent the story from being sufficiently worked out in terms of the characters; the characters, that is, are *in* the events, the events are not in them: we want a larger Englishman than Fielding, a weightier Indian than Aziz.

These are faults, it is true, and Forster is the one novelist who could commit them and yet transcend and even put them to use. The relation of the characters to the events, for example, is the result of a severe imbalance in the relation of plot to story. Plot and story in this novel are not coextensive as they are in all Forster's other novels.[4] The plot is precise, hard, crystallized and far simpler than any Forster has previously conceived. The story is beneath and above the plot and continues beyond it in time. It is, to be sure, created by the plot, it is the plot's manifold reverberation, but it is greater than the plot and contains it. The plot is as decisive as a judicial opinion; the story is an impulse, a tendency, a perception. The suspension of plot in the large circumambient sphere of story, the expansion of the story from the centre of plot, requires some of the subtlest manipulation that any novel has ever had. This relation of plot and story tells us that we are dealing with a political novel of an unusual kind. The characters are of sufficient size for the plot; they are not large enough for the story—and that indeed is the point of the story. . . .

[Summary of plot follows.]

Thus the plot. And no doubt it is too much a plot of event, too easily open and shut. Nevertheless it is an admirable if obvious device for organizing an enormous amount of observation of both English and native society; it brings to spectacular virulence the latent antagonisms between rulers and ruled.

Of the Anglo-Indian society it is perhaps enough to say that, "more

---

[4] I am not using plot and story in exactly the same sense that Forster uses them in *Aspects of the Novel.*

than it can hope to do in England," it lives by the beliefs of the English public school. It is arrogant, ignorant, insensitive—intelligent natives estimate that a year in India makes the pleasantest Englishman rude. And of all the English it is the women who insist most strongly on their superiority, who are the rawest and crudest in their manner. The men have a certain rough liking for the men of the subject race; for instance, Turton, Collector of the district, has "a contemptuous affection for the pawns he had moved about for so many years; they must be worth his pains." But the women, unchecked by any professional necessity or pride, think wholly in terms of the most elementary social prestige and Turton's wife lives for nothing else. " 'After all,' " Turton thinks but never dares say, " 'it's our women who make everything more difficult out here.' "

This is the result of the undeveloped heart. *A Passage to India* is not a radical novel; its data were gathered in 1912 and 1922, before the full spate of Indian nationalism; it is not concerned to show that the English should not be in India at all. Indeed, not until the end of the book is the question of the expulsion of the English mentioned, and the novel proceeds on an imperialistic premise— ironically, for it is not actually Forster's own—its chief point being that by reason of the undeveloped heart the English have thrown away the possibility of holding India. For want of a smile an Empire is to be lost.[5] Not even justice is enough. " 'Indians know whether they are liked or not,' " Fielding says, " '—they cannot be fooled here. Justice never satisfies them, and that is why the British Empire rests on sand.' " Mrs. Moore listens to Ronny defending the British attitude; "his words without his voice might have impressed her, but when she heard the self-satisfied lilt of them, when she saw the mouth moving so complacently and competently beneath the little red nose, she felt, quite illogically, that this was not the last word on India.

---

[5] H. N. Brailsford in his *Rebel India* (1931) deals at some length with the brutality with which demonstrations were put down in 1930. "Here and there," he says, "mildness and good-temper disarmed the local agitation. I heard of one magistrate, very popular with the people, who successfully treated the defiance of the Salt Monopoly as a joke. The local Congress leaders made salt openly in front of his bungalow. He came out: bought some of the contraband salt: laughed at its bad quality: chaffed the bystanders, and went quietly back to his house. The crowd melted away, and no second attempt was made to defy this genial bureaucrat. On the other hand, any exceptional severity, especially if physical brutality accompanied it, usually raised the temper of the local movement and roused it to fresh daring and further sacrifices."

One touch of regret—not the canny substitute but the true regret—
would have made him a different man, and the British Empire a
different institution."

Justice is not enough then, but in the end neither are liking and
goodwill enough. For although Fielding and Aziz reach out to each
other in friendship, a thousand little tricks of speech, a thousand different assumptions and different tempi keep them apart. They do not
understand each other's *amounts* of emotion, let alone kinds of emotion. " 'Your emotions never seem in proportion to their objects,
Aziz,' " Fielding says, and Aziz answers, " 'Is emotion a sack of pota-
toes, so much the pound, to be measured out?' "

The theme of separateness, of fences and barriers, the old theme of
the Pauline epistles, which runs through all Forster's novels, is, in
A Passage to India, hugely expanded and everywhere dominant. The
separation of race from race, sex from sex, culture from culture, even
of man from himself, is what underlies every relationship. The
separation of the English from the Indians is merely the most dramatic
of the chasms in this novel. Hindu and Moslem cannot really approach each other; Aziz, speaking in all friendliness to Professor Godbole, wishes that Hindus did not remind him of cow-dung and Professor Godbole thinks, " 'Some Moslems are very violent' "—"Between
people of distant climes there is always the possibility of romance,
but the various branches of Indians know too much about each other
to surmount the unknowable easily." Adela and Ronny cannot meet
in sexuality, and when, after the trial, Adela and Fielding meet in an
idea, "a friendliness, as of dwarfs shaking hands, was in the air."
Fielding, when he marries Mrs. Moore's daughter Stella, will soon
find himself apart from his young wife. And Mrs. Moore is separated
from her son, from all people, from God, from the universe.

This sense of separateness broods over the book, pervasive, symbolic
—at the end the very earth requires, and the sky approves, the parting
of Aziz and Fielding—and perhaps accounts for the remoteness of the
characters: they are so far from each other that they cannot reach
us. But the isolation is not merely adumbrated; in certain of its
aspects it is very precisely analysed and some of the most brilliant
and virtuose parts of the novel are devoted to the delineation of Aziz
and his friends, to the investigation of the cultural differences that
keep Indian and Englishman apart.

The mould for Aziz is Gino Carella of the first novel [*Where
Angels Fear to Tread*]. It is the mould of unEnglishness, that is to
say, of volatility, tenderness, sensibility, a hint of cruelty, much

warmth, a love of pathos, the desire to please even at the cost of insincerity. Like Gino's, Aziz's nature is in many ways child-like, in many ways mature: it is mature in its acceptance of child-like inconsistency. Although eager to measure up to English standards of puritan rectitude, Aziz lives closer to the literal facts of his emotions; for good or bad, he is more human. He, like his friends, is not prompt, not efficient, not neat, not really convinced of Western ideas even in science—when he retires to a native state he slips back to mix a little magic with his medicine—and he, like them, is aware of his faults. He is hyper-sensitive, imagining slights even when there are none because there have actually been so many; he is full of humility and full of contempt and desperately wants to be liked. He is not heroic but his heroes are the great chivalrous emperors, Babur and Alamgir. In short, Aziz is a member of a subject race. A rising nationalism in India may by now have thrust him aside in favour of a more militant type; but we can be sure that if the new type has repudiated Aziz's emotional contradictions it has not resolved them.

Aziz and his friends are Moslems, and with Moslems of the business and professional class the plot of the novel deals almost entirely. But the story is suffused with Hinduism.[6] It is Mrs. Moore who carries the Hindu theme; it is Mrs. Moore, indeed, who is the story. The theme is first introduced by Mrs. Moore observing a wasp.

> Going to hang up her cloak she found that the tip of the peg was occupied by a small wasp. . . . There he clung, asleep, while jackals in the plain bayed their desires and mingled with the percussion of drums.
>   "Pretty dear," said Mrs. Moore to the wasp. He did not wake, but her voice floated out, to swell the night's uneasiness.

This wasp is to recur in Professor Godbole's consciousness when he has left Chandrapore and taken service as director of education in a Hindu native state. He stands, his school quite forgotten—turned into a granary, indeed—and celebrates the birth of Krishna in the great religious festival that dominates the third part of the novel.[7]

[6] The Indian masses appear only as crowds in the novel; they have no individualized representative except the silent, unthinking figure of the man who pulls the *punkah* in the courtroom scene. He is one of the "untouchables" though he has the figure of a god, and in Adela's mind, just before the crisis of the trial, he raises doubts of the "suburban Jehovah" who sanctifies her opinions, and he makes her think of Mrs. Moore.

[7] The novel is divided: I. Mosque, II. Caves, III. Temple. In his notes to the Everyman edition Forster points out that the three parts correspond to the three Indian seasons. [I.e., Cold Weather, Hot Weather, and Rains.]

The wasp is mixed up in his mind—he does not know how it got there in the first place, nor do we—with a recollection of Mrs. Moore.

> He was a Brahman, she a Christian, but it made no difference, it made no difference whether she was a trick of his memory or a telepathic appeal. It was his duty, as it was his desire, to place himself in the position of the God and to love her, and to place himself in her position and say to the God: "Come, come, come, come." This was all he could do. How inadequate! But each according to his own capacities, and he knew that his own were small. "One old Englishwoman and one little, little wasp," he thought, as he stepped out of the temple into the grey of a pouring wet morning. "It does not seem much, still it is more than I am myself."

The presence of the wasp, first in Mrs. Moore's consciousness, then in Godbole's, Mrs. Moore's acceptance of the wasp, Godbole's acceptance of Mrs. Moore—in some symbolic fashion, this is the thread of the story of the novel as distinguished from its plot. For the story is essentially concerned with Mrs. Moore's discovery that Christianity is not adequate. In a quiet way, Mrs. Moore is a religious woman; at any rate, as she has grown older she has found it "increasingly difficult to avoid" mentioning God's name "as the greatest she knew." Yet in India God's name becomes less and less efficacious—"outside the arch there seemed always another arch, beyond the remotest echo a silence."

And so, unwittingly, Mrs. Moore has moved closer and closer to Indian ways of feeling. When Ronny and Adela go for an automobile ride with the Nawab Bahadur and the chauffeur swerves at something in the path and wrecks the car, Mrs. Moore, when she is told of the incident, remarks without thinking, " 'A ghost!' " And a ghost it was, or so the Nawab believed, for he had run over and killed a drunken man at that spot nine years before. "None of the English knew of this, nor did the chauffeur; it was a racial secret communicable more by blood than by speech." This "racial secret" has somehow been acquired by Mrs. Moore. And the movement away from European feeling continues: "She felt increasingly (vision or nightmare?) that, though people are important, the relations between them are not, and that in particular too much fuss has been made over marriage; centuries of carnal embracement, yet man is no nearer to understanding man." The occasion of her visit to the Marabar Caves is merely the climax of change, although a sufficiently terrible one.

What so frightened Mrs. Moore in the cave was an echo. It is but one echo in a book which is contrived of echoes. Not merely does

Adela Quested's delusion go in company with a disturbing echo in her head which only ceases when she masters her delusion, but the very texture of the story is a reticulation of echoes. Actions and speeches return, sometimes in a better, sometimes in a worse form, given back by the perplexing "arch" of the Indian universe. The recurrence of the wasp is a prime example, but there are many more. If Aziz plays a scratch game of polo with a subaltern who comes to think well of this particular anonymous native, the same subaltern will be particularly virulent in his denunciation of Aziz the rapist, never knowing that the liked and the detested native are the same. If the natives talk about their inability to catch trains, an Englishman's missing a train will make all the trouble of the story. Mrs. Moore will act with bad temper to Adela and with surly indifference to Aziz, but her action will somehow have a good echo; and her children will be her further echo. However we may interpret Forster's intention in this web of reverberation, it gives his book a cohesion and intricacy usually only found in music. And of all the many echoes, the dominant one is the echo that booms through the Marabar cave.

A Marabar cave had been horrid as far as Mrs. Moore was concerned, for she had nearly fainted in it, and had some difficulty in preventing herself from saying so as soon as she got into the air again. It was natural enough; she had always suffered from faintness, and the cave had become too full, because all their retinue followed them. Crammed with villagers and servants, the circular chamber began to smell. She lost Aziz and Adela in the dark, didn't know who touched her, couldn't breathe, and some vile naked thing struck her face and settled on her mouth like a pad. She tried to regain the entrance tunnel, but an influx of villagers swept her back. She hit her head. For an instant she went mad, hitting and gasping like a fanatic. For not only did the crush and stench alarm her; there was also a terrifying echo.

Professor Godbole had never mentioned an echo; it never impressed him, perhaps. There are some exquisite echoes in India; . . . The echo in a Marabar cave is not like these, it is entirely devoid of distinction. Whatever is said, the same monotonous noise replies, and quivers up and down the walls until it is absorbed in the roof. "Boum" is the sound as far as the human alphabet can express it, or "bou-oum," or "ou-boum"—utterly dull. Hope, politeness, the blowing of a nose, the squeal of a boot, all produce "boum."

Panic and emptiness—Mrs. Moore's panic had been at the emptiness of the universe. And one goes back beyond Helen Schlegel's experience of the Fifth Symphony in *Howards End:* the negating mess of the cave reminds us of and utterly denies the mess of that room in which

Caroline Abbott saw Gino with his child. For then the mess had been the source of life and hope, and in it the little child had blossomed; Caroline had looked into it from the "charnel chamber" of the reception room and the "light in it was soft and large, as from some gracious, noble opening." It is, one might say, a representation of the womb and a promise of life. There is also a child in the mess of the Marabar cave—for the "vile, naked thing" that settles "like a pad" on Mrs. Moore's mouth is "a poor little baby, astride its mother's hip." The cave's opening is behind Mrs. Moore, she is facing into the grave; light from the world does not enter, and the universe of death makes all things alike, even life and death, even good and evil.

> . . . The echo began in some indescribable way to undermine her hold on life. . . . It had managed to murmur: "Pathos, piety, courage—they exist, but are identical, and so is filth. Everything exists, nothing has value." If one had spoken of vileness in that place, or quoted lofty poetry, the comment would have been the same—"ou-boum." If one had spoken with the tongues of angels and pleaded for all the unhappiness and misunderstanding in the world, past, present, and to come; for all the misery men must undergo whatever their opinion and position, and however much they dodge or bluff—it would amount to the same. . . . Devils are of the north, and poems can be written about them, but no one could romanticize the Marabar because it robbed infinity and eternity of their vastness, the only quality that accommodates them to mankind. . . . But suddenly at the edge of her mind, religion reappeared, poor little talkative Christianity, and she knew that all its divine words from "Let there be Light" to "It is finished" only amounted to "boum."

"Something snub-nosed, incapable of generosity" had spoken to her —"the undying worm itself." Converse with God, her children, Aziz, is repugnant to her. She wants attention for her sorrow and rejects it when given. Knowing Aziz to be innocent, she says nothing in his behalf except a few sour words that upset Adela's certainty, and though she knows that her testimony will be useful to Aziz, she allows Ronny to send her away. She has had the beginning of the Hindu vision of things and it has crushed her. What the Hindu vision is, is expressed by Professor Godbole to Fielding:

> Good and evil are different, as their names imply. But, in my own humble opinion, they are both of them aspects of my Lord. He is present in the one, absent in the other, and the difference between presence and absence is great, as great as my feeble mind can grasp. Yet absence implies presence, absence is not non-existence, and we are therefore entitled to repeat: "Come, come, come, come."

Although Mrs. Moore abandons everything, even moral duty, she dominates the subsequent action. As "Esmiss Esmoor" she becomes, to the crowd around the courthouse, a Hindu goddess who was to save Aziz. And, we are vaguely given to understand, it is her influence that brings Adela to her senses and the truth. She recurs again, together with the wasp, in the mind of Professor Godbole in that wonderful scene of religious muddlement with which the book draws to its conclusion. She remains everlastingly in the mind of Aziz who hates —or tries to hate—all the other English. She continues into the future in her daughter Stella, who marries Fielding and returns to India, and in her son Ralph. Both Stella and Ralph "like Hinduism, though they take no interest in its forms" and are shy of Fielding because he thinks they are mistaken. Despite the sullen disillusionment in which Mrs. Moore died, she had been right when she had said to Ronny that there are many kinds of failure, some of which succeed. No thought, no deed in this book of echoes, is ever lost.

It is not easy to know what to make of the dominant Hinduism of the third section of the novel. The last part of the story is frankly a coda to the plot, a series of resolutions and separations which comment on what has gone before—in it Fielding and Aziz meet and part, this time for ever; Aziz forgives Adela Quested and finds a friend in Ralph Moore; Fielding, we learn, is not really at one with his young wife; Hindu and Moslem, Brahman and non-Brahman are shown to be as far apart as Indian and English, yet English and Moslem meet in the flooded river, in a flow of Hindu religious fervour; and everything is encompassed in the spirit of Mrs. Moore, mixed up with a vision of the ultimate nullity, with the birth of Krishna and with joy in the fertile rains.

Certainly it is not to be supposed that Forster finds in Hinduism an answer to the problem of India; and its dangers have been amply demonstrated in the case of Mrs. Moore herself. But here at least is the vision in which the arbitrary human barriers sink before the extinction of all things. About seventy-five years before *A Passage to India*, Matthew Arnold's brother, William Delafield Arnold, went out to India as Director of Public Education of the Punjab. From his experiences he wrote a novel, *Oakfield: Or, Fellowship in the East*; it was a bitter work which denounced the English for making India a "rupee mine" and it declared that the "grand work" of civilizing India was all humbug. William Arnold thought that perhaps socialism, but more likely the Church of England, could bring about some change. This good and pious man felt it "grievous to live among

men"—the Indians—"and feel the idea of fraternity thwarted by
facts"; he believed that "we must not resign ourselves, without a
struggle, to calling the Indians brutes." To such a pass has Christianity
come, we can suppose Forster to be saying. We must suffer a vision
even as dreadful as Mrs. Moore's if by it the separations can be wiped
out. But meanwhile the separations exist and Aziz in an hysteria of
affirmation declares to Fielding on their last ride that the British
must go, even at the cost of internal strife, even if it means a Japanese
conquest. Only with the British gone can he and Fielding be friends.
Fielding offers friendship now: " 'It's what I want. It's what you
want.' " But the horses, following the path the earth lays for them,
swerve apart; earth and sky seem to say that the time for friendship
has not come, and leave its possibility to events.

The disintegrating question, What, then, must be done? which
many readers have raised is of course never answered—or not answered in the language in which the question has been asked. The
book simply involves the question in ultimates. This, obviously, is no
answer; still, it defines the scope of a possible answer, and thus re-
states the question. For the answer can never again temporize, because the question, after it has been involved in the moods and
visions of the story, turns out to be the most enormous question that
has ever been asked, requiring an answer of enormous magnanimity.
Great as the problem of India is, Forster's book is not about India
alone; it is about all of human life.

A Passage to India Reconsidered

by Walter A. S. Keir

"I describe not the essence but the passage."

Montaigne

What is still a far too common approach to *A Passage to India* is admirably if obliquely indicated by some of Forster's own comments on Conrad's *Notes on Life and Letters,* as these are quoted by F. R. Leavis in *The Great Tradition.* "What is so elusive about him," Leavis quotes, "is that he is always promising to make some general philosophic statement about the universe, and then refraining with a gruff disclaimer. . . . Is there not also a central obscurity, something noble, heroic, beautiful, inspiring half a dozen great books, but obscure, obscure? . . . These essays do suggest that he is misty in the middle as well as at the edges, that the secret casket of his genius contains a vapour rather than a jewel; and that we needn't try to write him down philosophically, because there is, in this direction, nothing to write. No creed, in fact. Only opinions, and the right to throw them overboard when facts make them look absurd. Opinions held under the semblance of eternity, girt with the sea, crowned with the stars, and therefore easily mistaken for a creed." Here, it might be thought at first sight, Forster is criticising something of which he himself is guilty. For is there not, by the standards implied here, a "central obscurity" in *A Passage to India* itself? And are there not, notoriously, several other incidental obscurities as well? What really happened to Miss Quested in the caves, for example? What is the purpose of the wasps which intrude periodically in the characters' thoughts? What was the real cause of the accident to the Nawab Bahadur's car? What is the exact point of Mrs. Moore's echo of

"A Passage to India *Reconsidered" by Walter A. S. Keir. From* Cambridge Journal *5 (1951–52): 426–35. Copyright April 1952. Reprinted by permission of Bowes and Bowes, Publishers, Ltd.*

"Ou-Boum," or of Professor Godbole's reiterated cry of "Come, come, come . . ."? What is the meaning of the whole of the final section, "The Temple"? "What is its spiritual side, if it has one?" as Fielding asks.

What, in fact, is "the final message of India" and of this novel? These are questions which have been asked ever since the book was published, and they will continue to be asked wherever the rhetorical interpretation of literature is preferred to what is loosely called the aesthetic. Yet Forster himself, of course, aligns himself wholeheartedly with the latter point of view, and for evidence of this we need look no further than at one of the sentences omitted by Dr. Leavis from the passage quoted above for his own sufficient (and sufficiently obvious) reasons. For in the original essay, as it is printed in *Abinger Harvest,* after "but obscure, obscure . . ." occurs the all-important qualification: "While reading the half-dozen books one *doesn't* or *shouldn't* [my italics] ask such a question, but it occurs, not improperly, when the author professes to be personal, and to take us into that confidence of his" i.e. when writing not as a novelist, but as an essayist. The exclusion of this reservation by Dr. Leavis, and its presence in Forster's original, indicate in an interesting fashion their respective positions. Dr. Leavis, plainly, is unwilling, here at least, to distinguish between the author speaking as an individual, and the author speaking as an artist. While to Forster, equally plainly, the two activities are separate, and demand very different methods of approach. Most novelists would, of course, support Forster. Conrad himself, for example, has answered the criticism implicit in the former attitude where he writes that "Liberty of imagination should be the most precious possession of a novelist. To try voluntarily to discover the fettering dogmas of some romantic, realistic, or naturalistic creed in the free work of its own inspiration is a trick worthy of human perverseness which, after inventing an absurdity, endeavours to find for it a pedigree of distinguished ancestors." Many others could be similarly quoted, right down, oddly enough, to Priestley, with Hardy most succinct of all where he writes "A novel is an impression, not an argument." But the main point here is not to prove one theory or the other, or even to weigh the evidence on either side. It is to make sure that we shall approach *A Passage to India* as Forster wishes us to approach it, primarily, that is to say, as a work of art or as an impression, and only secondarily as an argument or a political tract or a social document. He himself is quite explicit on this point in *Aspects of the Novel*—strangely neglected by critics of his own works—in "The Raison D'Etre of Criticism in the Arts" and in "Art for Art's sake." [1] "Art for art's sake?" he asks in the last of these, "I should just think so and more so than ever at the present time. It is the one orderly product which our muddling race has produced. It is the cry of a thousand sentinels, the echo from a thousand labyrinths, it is the lighthouse that cannot be hidden; *c'est le meilleur témoignage que nous puissions donner de notre dignité*."

We are not, then, to read *A Passage to India* in the hope of finding in it either a clear-cut and comprehensive "philosophy," or a ready made solution for the problems of its characters, though on certain levels (and like all Forster's novels this book is constructed level upon level, depth upon depth), the issues are abundantly clear. This is true both of the "story," in the narrow sense of the word, and of the political implications of the English in India, "so cold and odd and circulating like an ice stream" through this land they so lamentably misunderstand, implications well enough indicated by Forster's comment in an essay in the *Nation and Athenaeum* that "never in history did ill breeding contribute so much to the dissolution of an Empire." Rich and subtle as Forster is in these respects, it is not this "passage," a passage by 1st Class P. and O. to the clubs and residences of the British Raj which is our primary concern. Rather it is that "Passage" of Whitman's poem from which Forster takes his title, the "passage to more than India," the

Passage, indeed, O Soul to primal thought,
Not lands and seas alone, thy own clear freshness,
The young maturity of brood and bloom,
To realms of budding bibles.

the

Passage to you, you shores, ye aged fierce enigmas,
Passage to you, to mastership of you, ye strangling problems,
You, strewed with the wrecks of skeletons, that, living, never reached you.

the "passage" leading to the fundamental question,

What is this separate nature so unnatural,
What is this earth to our affections (unloving earth,
without a throb to answer ours, Cold earth, the place of graves)?

This, primarily, is the passage now taken by Forster. And like Whitman he is supremely conscious of its mystery, its unnaturalness.

[1] Originally published in *Horizon* and reprinted in *Two Cheers for Democracy*.

"The Mediterranean," he writes, is "the human norm, it is the harmony between the works of man and the earth that upholds them, the civilization that has escaped muddle, the spirit in a reasonable form, with flesh and blood subsisting." But, he goes on, "when men leave that exquisite lake, whether through the Bosphorus or the Pillars of Hercules, they approach the monstrous and the extraordinary; and the southern exit leads to the strangest experience of all." "The *strangest* experience of all"—it is this he attempts to convey, the mystery of India, its complexity, its lack of form, its lack of meaning. This can only be done impressionistically, by suggestion.

This, in fact, is what we find throughout. "Nothing embraces the whole of India," Aziz insists, "Nothing, nothing!" And thus while much of the action takes place in the civil station of Chandrapore, we are constantly reminded that Chandrapore is not "India," that "India is the country, fields, fields, then hills, jungle, hills and more fields. The branch line stops, the road is only practicable for cars up to a point, the bullocks lumber down the side tracks, paths fray out into the cultivation and disappear near a splash of red paint." While along with this conception of a vast, mysterious hinterland goes automatically the conception of its uncounted and uncountable inhabitants. "He had spoken in the little room near the court where the pleaders wait for their clients," Forster writes of one of the characters after the invitations to the "bridge party" have gone out. "Clients, waiting for pleaders, sat in the dust outside. And there were circles even beyond these—people who wore nothing but a loin cloth, people who wore not even that, and spent their lives knocking two sticks together before a scarlet doll, humanity drifting and grading until no earthly invitation can embrace it." There is always in this book the suggestion of something beyond and beyond again, "outside the arch always another arch, beyond the remotest arch a silence," arches ascending in ever increasing size from those of black polished nothingness, which are the Marabar Caves, to that which overarches all the skies in the famous "Bridge party" scene. This half-tragic, half-comic scene is completely characteristic of Forster's vision, as he shows us the two pathetic ranks of English and Indians, each drawn up at its own side of the club lawn, each acutely conscious of the petty but "unbridgeable" gulf between them, but both ignoring the immense frame in which they stand and its ironic, unspoken commentary. "Some kites," Forster writes, "hovered overhead, impartial, over the kites passed the mass of a vulture, and with an impartiality exceeding all, the sky not deeply coloured, but translucent, poured light from its whole circumference. It seemed unlikely that the series stopped there. Beyond the sky must there not be always something that overarches all the skies, beyond which again . . . ?" Impersonality, space, this is the atmosphere, and permeating all, with only rare exceptions, is disillusionment. "In Europe," Forster writes, "life retreats out of the cold, and beautiful fireside myths have resulted—Balder, Persephone—but here the retreat is from the source of life itself, the treacherous sun, and no poetry adorns it, because disillusionment cannot be beautiful. Men yearn for poetry though they may not confess it; they desire that joy shall be graceful and sorrow august and infinity have a form, and India fails to accommodate them." "How can the mind take hold of such a country?" Forster finally asks. "Generations of invaders have tried, but they remain in exile." And how, too, it might be asked, should any critic try, as many have done, to follow to some preconceived goal paths that "fray out . . . and disappear near a splash of red paint"? How define a meaning that is no meaning? They cannot, nor is there any reason why they should attempt it. All Forster asks is that we apprehend this atmosphere imaginatively.

Our approach to the action on the levels where it now concerns us, to the action, that is, as it is involved in the questions asked earlier—this should be along similar lines. For again *A Passage to India* does not offer a clear-cut, logical chain of events, subservient to the laws of cause and effect, so much as a complex pattern shadowed against this profound and disquieting background, modifying it, and in turn being modified. Yet certain pointers for our understanding do of course emerge—with regard to Mrs. Moore's experience of the echo in the Marabar Caves, for example. "Coming at a time when she chanced to be fatigued," Forster writes, "it had managed to murmur, 'Pathos, piety, courage—they exist, but are identical, and so is filth. Everything exists, nothing has value.' If one had spoken vileness in that place, or quoted lofty poetry, the comment would have been the same—'ou-boum' . . . But suddenly at the edge of her mind religion appeared, poor little talkative Christianity, and she knew that all its divine words from 'Let there be Light' to 'It is finished' only amounted to 'boum.' Then she was terrified over an area larger than usual; the universe, never comprehensible to her intellect, offered no repose to her soul; the mood of the last two months took definite form at last, and she realized that she didn't want to write to her children, didn't want to communicate with anyone, not even with God." Now there is no real reason why this should not be accepted as the possible, if unusual, experience of one old lady suddenly transplanted to a new and incomprehensible world. Yet because it strikes an altogether new note in Forster—the temporary depression of George Emerson in *A Room With a View* is not strictly comparable —because of this, and because it, quite deliberately, suggests more than it says, critics have attempted to find some sort of justification for this experience, philosophical or otherwise, and have become petulant when, naturally, they have failed to do so.

Some have even suggested that it represents Forster's own point of view. Nothing, of course, could be more absurd, for we know, and can confirm from his personal writings such as *What I Believe*,[2] exactly where Forster stands, and it is obviously not with Mrs. Moore. What is implicit in the above, however, is a criticism of "poor, little, talkative Christianity," and in particular of the inadequacy of England's drawing room religion when confronted by such a phenomenon as India. This theme occurs elsewhere also—in the delightful description of the singing of "God Save The King" at the club, for example—and later finds its fullest expression in the behaviour of Miss Quested during the trial. For although in the privacy and security of her room in the heart of Anglo-India she has prayed for a favourable verdict, believing that "God who saves the King will surely support the police," when she actually confronts the court she wonders, "In virtue of what had she collected this roomful of people together? Her particular brand of opinions, and the suburban Jehovah who sanctified them—by what right did they claim so much importance in the world, and assume the title of civilization?" But what is merely chastening to Miss Quested, for a long time a non-practising Christian, is fatal to the aged Mrs. Moore. Nor is there anything particularly sudden in her assumption of despair. "God," Forster writes, "had been constantly in her thoughts since she entered India, though oddly he satisfied her less and less. She must needs pronounce his name as the greatest that she knew, yet she had never found it less efficacious. Outside the arch there always seemed another arch . . ." Always Forster brings us back to this. Circumference impinges on centre, centre on circumference.

Mrs. Moore's attitude of negation, in any case, is accurately balanced by that of Professor Godbole. Informed of the "attack" on Miss Quested he is obtuse about it for some time, and then comes as far into the open as we expect of him. "I am informed," he says,

---

[2] Reprinted in *Two Cheers for Democracy*.

"that an evil action was performed in the Marabar hills . . . My answer to that is this! That action was performed by Dr. Aziz." He stopped and sucked in his thin cheeks. "It was performed by the guide." He stopped again. "It was performed by you." Now he had an air of daring and of coyness. "It was performed by me." He looked shyly down the sleeve of his coat. "And by my students. It was even performed by the lady herself. When evil occurs it expresses the whole of the universe. Similarly when good occurs!" But "Good and evil" he goes on, after Fielding has protested that he is preaching that good and evil are the same, "good and evil are different as their names imply. But in my own humble opinion they are both of them aspects of my Lord. He is present in the one, absent in the other, and the difference between absence and presence is great, as great as my feeble mind can grasp. Yet absence implies presence, absence is not non-existence, and we are therefore entitled to repeat 'Come, come, come.' " This, of course, as "philosophy" is sufficiently tenuous. But we are not here concerned with its absolute value. Our purpose is merely to notice Godbole's position with regard to Mrs. Moore. For to her good and evil *are* now the same. Hers, in fact, is the way of rejection of all things, and his, as we shall see more fully later, is the way of acceptance of all things. Neither is necessarily Forster's. He is concerned as a novelist to present these two as human beings with whatever truth or falsehood they may contain, for Forster's characters, it should be remembered, by their acts, their relationships, and their impact on one another, to a considerable extent reproduce in human terms the muddle and the incompleteness of India to which we have referred—or, it would be more accurate to say, the muddle and the incompleteness of life as it is here exaggerated to an extreme degree by differences of race, colour, creed, climate and thought. So far as his own position with regard to Godbole's "Come, come, come" is concerned, it is sufficiently indicated by his comment, "She [India] calls 'Come' through her hundred mouths, through objects ridiculous and august. But come to what? She has never defined. She is not a promise, only an appeal."

These two threads in the pattern are finally resolved in the last section of the book, "The Temple." Christianity, as we have seen, has been criticized as provincial. It has also been criticized earlier in the descriptions of the two missionaries, old Mr. Graysford and young Mr. Sorley, because it ignores, or discounts, large areas of life. Mr. Graysford, it will be remembered, will not allow monkeys to enter the kingdom of heaven, while Mr. Sorley, more advanced, still draws the line at wasps—wasps which are deliberately included, we find, in the meditations of both Mrs. Moore and Professor Godbole, partly for the reason indicated here, and partly for technical reasons, for what Forster in *Aspects of the Novel* calls "Rhythm." "And the wasps?" Forster writes of Sorley. "He became uneasy during the descent to wasps, and was apt to change the conversation. And oranges, cactuses, crystals, and mud? And the bacteria inside Mr. Sorley? No, no, this is going too far. We must exclude something or we shall be left with nothing." In the celebration of the festival of Gokal Ashtami, on the other hand, focal point of the whole of this last section, and the embodiment in ritual of the philosophy of Professor Godbole, nothing is left out. Completion is essential, "all spirit and all matter must participate in salvation." So when the clocks strike midnight "Infinite love took upon itself the form of Krishna and saved the world. All sorrow was annihilated, not only for Indians, but for foreigners, birds, caves, railways, and the stars." The suggestion being, then, that we can include everything, as Godbole does, or exclude everything, as Mrs. Moore does. There is only irony for the half-way house of old Mr. Graysford and young Mr. Sorley.

But the festival of Gokal Ashtami is also important for another reason. It is the celebration, as Forster points out, of the birth of Krishna, and it coincides to some extent with the comparable scenes at Bethlehem. (Similarly "The Temple" as a whole corresponds to the season of the rains, and consequently to rebirth, while "The Mosque" corresponds to the cold weather, and "The Caves" to the hot weather. They also appear to suggest three periods of Indian history,—the Moghul empires of the past, "present" Anglo-India, and a future predominantly Hindu, but one still with a place for such Moslems as Aziz.) This God, however, is "thrown away" after his immediate function is performed—he is to be understood as a momentary symbol, that is to say, and not in terms of a creed. But before he is thrown away, some of the characters, previously mere spectators, become to some extent at least participators. For as the tray with the tiny model of the village of Gokal is being pushed, burning, into the lake, the boats carrying Fielding, Aziz, Stella and Ralph collide with it. "The four outsiders flung out their arms and grappled, and, with oars and poles sticking out, revolved like a mythical monster in the whirlwind. The worshippers howled with wrath or joy, as they drifted helplessly against the servitor. Who awaited them, his beautiful dark face expressionless, and as the last morsels melted on the tray, it struck them. The shock was minute, but Stella, nearest to it, shrank into her husband's arms, then reached forward, then flung herself against Aziz, and her motions capsized them. They plunged into the warm shallow water, and rose struggling into a tornado of noise. The oars, the sacred tray, the letters of Ronny and Adela, broke loose and floated confusedly. Artillery was fired, drums beaten, the elephants trumpeted, and drowning all an immense peal of thunder, unaccompanied by lightning, cracked like a mallet on the dome."

This extract is rich in suggestions. It may suggest that the people in the boat partook, for a very brief moment, and at the actual second of the dissolution of the image, in this celebration in which "all sorrow was annihilated, not only for Indians but for foreigners . . ."—that they apprehended momentarily that "passage" of which Forster writes in his comment on the end of the God: "Thus was He thrown year after year, and were others thrown—little images of Ganpati, baskets of ten-day corn, tiny tazias after Mohurram—scapegoats, husks, emblems of passage; a passage not easy, not now, not here, not to be apprehended except when it is unattainable: the God to be thrown was an emblem of that." [3] Or they may actually have hastened the dissolution. One cannot be sure—"the worshippers howled with wrath *or* joy . . ." But in any case the apprehension, or the intrusion, is only momentary. This God offers no permanent solution to the world's troubles, is only cathartic, and immediately afterwards life returns to normal, the old inadequacies reassert themselves, and the book ends with the famous ride of Fielding and Aziz. " 'Why can't we be friends now?' " Fielding asks. " 'It's what I want. It's what you want.' But the horses didn't want it—they swerved apart; the earth didn't want it, sending up rocks through which the riders must pass single file; the temple, the tank, the jail, the palace, the birds, the carrion, the guest house

---

[3] [1969] Forster's comment, which I quote here, is one of the most explicit he makes, and seems to me central to an understanding of the novel as a whole. The propitiatory offerings of baskets of ten-day corn are self-explanatory. Ganpati is a Hindu god, and in many parts of India models of him are made, kept for a brief period, often only twenty-four hours, and then he is ritually "thrown away," into rivers, for example, or in coastal areas into the sea, to ward off evil spirits and to bring good fortune. A tazia, though significantly perhaps the word literally means consolation, is a model or representation of the tomb of Hasan and Husain. These are carried in procession after the Mohammedan festival of Mohurram, which commemorates the death of the Prophet's grandson, and they too are ritually "thrown away" into rivers or burnt. Forster also refers briefly to tazias in Chapter 21.

that came into view as they issued from the gap and saw Mau beneath, they didn't want it, they said in their hundred voices, 'No, not yet,' and the sky said, 'No, not here.' " Thus just as "foreigners, caves, railways, and the stars" participated in the union earlier, so now do all the above participate in the final separation.

But they "participate" obviously, in an imaginative sense and not in a literal one. For this is the second point brought out here more clearly even than elsewhere, the point made earlier that Forster is far more concerned with conveying a particular, and very beautiful, aesthetic effect than with an exact symbolism. "That was the climax" he comments after the collision of the boat and tray, "so far as India admits of one . . . Whatever had happened had happened. Looking back at the great blur of the last twenty-four hours, no man could say where was the emotional centre of it, any more than he could locate the heart of a cloud." Exactly the same is true of *A Passage to India* as a whole. It reflects many things in its profound and changing depths, but it offers no religious or mystical solution for the problems it propounds. For although Forster has a certain tenderness for religion, even this tenderness is for its aesthetic qualities rather than for its ethical or theological content. He is tender to it, as Trilling points out, because it expresses, though it does not solve, the human predicament, and because it is, after all, the supreme achievement in the search for "connection." And this is how he uses religion here, how indeed he uses the bulk of his material, to express the predicaments of his characters, but not to solve them, to create an impression, but not to argue.

That this is the case, then, we can confirm by appealing to what Forster has written elsewhere, in his criticism, and in the statements of his personal faith. But there are also many hints within the book itself, in addition to those already mentioned—hints that at first sight might appear to be quite unrelated to one another and to the main theme. There is, for example, the remark that Fielding "cares for truth of mood rather than for verbal truth." There is the account of the friends of Aziz, who, when he recited poetry to them, "listened delighted, for they took the public view of poetry, not the private which obtains in England. It never bored them to hear words, words: they breathed them with the cool night air, never stopping to analyse." Even the corrupt Police Inspector listens. He "did not . . . break into that cheery guffaw with which an Englishman averts the infection of beauty. He just sat with his mind empty, and when his thoughts, which were mainly ignoble, flowed back into it, they had a pleasant freshness." And there is finally the description of that Indian civiliza-tion "found not in great works of art or mighty deeds, but in the gestures well-bred Indians make when they sit or lie down. Fielding who had dressed up in native costume, learnt from his excessive awkwardness in it that all his motions were makeshifts, whereas when the Nawab Bahadur stretched out his hands for food, or Nureddin applauded a song, something beautiful had been accomplished which needed no development. This restfulness of gesture—it is the Peace that passeth Understanding, after all, it is the social equivalent of Yoga. When the whirring of action ceases, it becomes visible, and reveals a civilization which the West can disturb but can never acquire. The hand stretches out for ever, the lifted knee has the eternity though not the sadness of the grave." "Truth of mood rather than verbal truth," "words, words," "something beautiful had been accomplished which needed no development"—all of these are in-dications of one way to approach most works of art, but particularly how Forster wishes us to approach this work of art. Indeed he goes further. "We must come back to love," Forster writes in "The Raison D'Etre of Criticism": "That alone raises us to the co-operation with the artist which is the sole reason for our aesthetic pilgrimage. That alone promises spiritual parity." This may not always be true. But if it is true anywhere, it is true of *A Passage to India,* of all Forster's novels the one most concerned with "melody—or perception of the truth" (not, it should be noted, analysis of the truth), which in his most famous pronouncement on the novel he preferred to that "low atavistic form," the story. "Melody" here, moreover, may be under-stood almost literally, for as Burra noticed in his admirable essay on Forster, reprinted as the Introduction to the Everyman Edition, *A Passage to India* is very closely modelled on music. Patterned, harmonious, profound, the whole is bound together by the recurrent themes, the elusive, echoing melodies, and by that rhythm which with "its lovely waxing and waning fills us with surprise and freshness and hope." [4]

To some, of course, this will be unsatisfactory. They will accuse Forster of evasiveness, of replacing thought by sensibility, and they will refuse to recognize truth which he achieves as truth of any kind. They will continue, in fact, to demand their pound of flesh, their much desired "final message." If they do so, then as a last resort we can only indicate the mis-spelt inscription which presides over part

---

[4] The phrase is used by Forster himself, of Proust, in *Aspects of the Novel.*

of the Festival scene—"God si love." "God si love?" Forster himself asks. "Is this the final message of India?" This is unlikely to satisfy them. Yet it may not only be playfulness on Forster's part, for such is the virtue of his subtle and delicate art that even here it is possible to recognize something rather too uncomfortably apposite in this as a final message from a land of such desperate and pathetic muddle and confusion, of such spawning and incongruous piety, a suggestion that though God may well exist, there is yet something rather strange about him, something a little unexpected, something, even, a little absurd. But then life, as Philip discovered for Forster as early as *Where Angels Fear to Tread,* "Life, though greater than he supposed, was even less complete."

E. M. Forster: *A Passage to India*

by Arnold Kettle

Relationships often peter out in Forster's novels, as they do in life, and as they never seem to, for instance, in Lawrence. The contrast between the two writers is an obvious yet an interesting one: Lawrence so intense, Forster so continuously relaxed. Is not the relaxation, the sceptical sophistication, likely to lead to a certain passivity? In a way I think it does. One cannot imagine one of Lawrence's characters lapsing into wistfulness (one wishes from time to time they would); but in Forster there is perhaps a little too much of it. The refusal to be heroic may be very human but it is also less than human. The relationship between Fielding and Aziz comes to grief—if that is not too strong a word—in the way such a relationship would very likely come to grief. On the personal level that is convincing enough. The doubt in one's mind lies in the attempt of Forster to generalize on the basis of that relationship. If the last paragraph of the novel means anything at all it means that the answer to Mahmoud Ali's original question "whether or no it is possible to be friends with an Englishman?" is "No, not yet, no, not there." Not, that is, till the English have been driven out of India, when a friendship based on equality rather than imperialism will be possible. But might not friendship with Aziz have been possible had Fielding been prepared to go a little further, to renounce rather more than he was prepared to renounce of the imperialist attitude?

I think it is necessary to ask this question because Forster's failure to consider its possibility does something to his book. To attempt to sum up the final sense about life conveyed by *A Passage to India* one would have, I think, to turn towards some such phrases as "Ah yes, it's all very difficult. There aren't any easy short cuts. Let's try

Extract from "E. M. Forster: A Passage to India," in An Introduction to the English Novel *by Arnold Kettle (London: Hutchinson & Co. [Publishers], Ltd., 1953), Vol. 2, pp. 159–63. Reprinted by permission of the publisher.*

45

and be sensible and honest and unsentimental. Above all let's be
honest. And one day things will be a bit better no doubt." It is,
heaven knows, not an unsympathetic attitude, nor a valueless one,
and it is a thousand times better than the defeatism to which, since
A Passage to India, we have become accustomed. Yet it does, I suggest,
reveal a limitation in the assessment of the capacity of human beings
radically to change their consciousness. And this limitation reduces
the book somehow, and all Forster's books. "Donnish" someone has
called him, "spinsterish" someone else; "soft" is the word he has
used himself. Inadequate words, yet one sees what they mean.

The truth is that in his determination to avoid any kind of humbug Forster tends to underplay certain of the underlying issues in
life which often give rise to humbug but cannot be laughed away
by its exposure. Keats's famous remark about being sure of nothing
but the holiness of the heart's affections has a relevance to Forster.
(It is one of those odd chances which one suspects to be more than
chance that he should have named his chief English character as he
did—another Fielding was an urbane expounder of the values of the
heart.) There is an important episode in which Ronny Heaslop puts
the Anglo-Indian case to his mother, Mrs. Moore:

> ". . . I am out here to work, mind, to hold this wretched country
> by force. I'm not a missionary or a Labour member or a vague senti-
> mental sympathetic literary man. I'm just a servant of the Govern-
> ment; it's the profession you wanted me to choose myself, and that's
> that. We're not pleasant in India, and we don't intend to be pleasant.
> We've something more important to do."
>
> He spoke sincerely. Every day he worked hard in the court trying to
> decide which of two untrue accounts was the less untrue, trying to dis-
> pense justice fearlessly, to protect the weak against the less weak, the
> incoherent against the plausible, surrounded by lies and flattery. That
> morning he had convicted a railway clerk of over-charging pilgrims for
> their tickets, and a Pathan of attempted rape. He expected no gratitude,
> no recognition for this, and both clerk and Pathan might appeal, bribe
> their witnesses more effectually in the interval, and get their sentences
> reversed. It was his duty. But he did expect sympathy from his own
> people, and except from newcomers he obtained it. He did think he
> ought not to be worried about "Bridge Parties" when the day's work
> was over and he wanted to play tennis with his equals or rest his legs
> upon a long chair.
>
> He spoke sincerely, but she could have wished with less gusto. How
> Ronny revelled in the drawbacks of his situation! How he did rub it in

that he was not in India to behave pleasantly, and derived positive
satisfaction therefrom! He reminded her of his public-schooldays. The
traces of young-man humanitarianism had sloughed off, and he talked
like an intelligent and embittered boy. His words without his voice
might have impressed her, but when she heard the self-satisfied lilt of
them, when she saw the mouth moving so complacently and competently
beneath the little red nose, she felt, quite illogically that this was not
the last word on India. One touch of regret—not the canny substitute
but the true regret from the heart—would have made him a different
man, and the British Empire a different institution.[1]

It is in the final sentence that Forster lets us down and exposes the
weaknesses of his positive values. It is simply not true that one
touch of genuine regret would have made the British Empire a
different institution and it is this kind of inadequacy which gives
rise to D. S. Savage's comment (in an essay which seems to me, by
and large, very unjust) on *A Passage to India.*

> . . . The ugly realities underlying the presence of the British in India
> are not even glanced at and the issues raised are handled as though
> they could be solved on the surface level of personal intercourse and
> individual behaviour.[2]

The reply to this is, of course, that Forster is writing a novel about
personal intercourse and not a tract about the political situation;
it is not an entirely convincing reply because Forster by his own
constant movement from the individual to the general, so clearly
recognizes that the two are subtly intertwined. It is, for instance, a
weakness of the novelist and not merely of the social thinker, that one
should constantly feel that Forster hates the public schools more
than he hates what gives rise to them.

Another result of the unsatisfactoriness of Forster's positives is
the element of mistiness involved in his treatment of Mrs. Moore.
It is difficult to isolate precisely this element. The presentation of
Mrs. Moore bristles with "significance." It is she who first makes
contact with Aziz in the mosque. It is she who for some time appears
to be bridging the gap between East and West. Then, in the first
of the Marabar caves, she undergoes a psychic experience or vision—
brought about by the dead, hostile echo of the cave—which destroys
her sincere but rather tenuous Christianity but leaves her exhausted

[1] *A Passage to India,* Ch. V.
[2] D. S. Savage, *The Withered Branch,* London, 1950, p. 47.

and passive. Although she believes Aziz to be innocent she allows
herself to be sent away before she can testify on his behalf. On the
Indian Ocean she dies; it has been for her a one-way passage.

Mrs. Moore, living and dead, plays an important part in the novel.
One cannot but associate her to some degree with Mrs. Ramsay in
To the Lighthouse and that other figure who so closely resembles
Mrs. Ramsay, Mrs. Wilcox in *Howards End*. These women are all
envisaged as somehow deep in the flux of things, associated with the
processes of nature, at one in some profound intuitive way with the
mysteries of the universe. They might be regarded, I think, as
twentieth-century versions of the archetypal Mother.

Mrs. Moore's vision is connected (partly through the image of the
wasp which is significant both to her and Professor Godbole) with
Hinduism, though it is hard to say just how. What the Mrs. Moore-
Hindu theme in *A Passage to India* really amounts to, I think, is an
attempt by Forster, the liberal agnostic, to get beyond his own scepti-
cism. There is a very interesting passage in which Fielding and Miss
Quested, both individualists and sceptics, discuss how Mrs. Moore
could have known what happened to Miss Quested in the cave. The
girl suggests the obvious "scientific" explanation—telepathy.

> The pert, meagre word fell to the ground. Telepathy? What an ex-
> planation! Better withdraw it, and Adela did so. She was at the end of
> her spiritual tether, and so was he. Were there worlds beyond which
> they could never touch, or did all that is possible enter their conscious-
> ness? They could not tell. They only realized that their outlook was
> more or less similar, and found in this a satisfaction. Perhaps life is a
> mystery, not a muddle; they could not tell. Perhaps the hundred Indias
> which fuss and squabble so tiresomely are one, and the universe they
> mirror is one. They had not the apparatus for judging.[3]

Is there not here Forster's own voice speaking? It is as though
he is conscious at some level or other of the limitations of his own
philosophy in which there is no room for a whole that is somehow
greater than the sum of the parts and which constantly sidetracks
his attempts at generalization. The weakness of all Forster's novels
lies in a failure to dramatize quite convincingly the positive values
which he has to set against the destroyers of the morality of the heart.
In *Howards End* he lapses into a rather half-hearted paean in praise
of country life and the yeoman stock in whom lies Britain's hope.

[3] *Op. cit.,* Ch. XXIX.

In *A Passage to India* the weakness lies in a certain vagueness sur-
rounding the Mrs. Moore-Professor Godbole material.

One might put it another way. Forster uses Mrs. Moore and the
Hindu theme to attempt to achieve a dimension of which he feels
the necessity but for which his liberal agnosticism has no place. But
because he is sceptical about the very material he is using he fails
to give it that concrete artistic force which alone could make it play
an effective part in the novel's pattern. Such passages as the twelfth
chapter of the novel in which Hinduism is seen historically and a
wonderful sense of age and mutability is achieved by "placing" India
geologically, are completely successful. But when Forster attempts to
give to Mrs. Moore a kind of significance which his own method
has already undermined then the novel stumbles. The distinction
between mystery and muddle itself becomes uneasy. The agnostic
attempt to get the best of both worlds, to undermine mysticism
without rejecting it, lies behind the difficulty.

And yet the tentativeness, the humility of Forster's attitude is
not something to undervalue. The "perhapses" that lie at the core
of his novels, constantly pricking the facile generalization, hinting
at the unpredictable element in the most fully analysed relationship,
cannot be brushed aside as mere liberal pusillanimity. He seems to
me a writer of scrupulous intelligence, of tough and abiding insights,
who has never been afraid of the big issues or the difficult ones and
has scorned to hide his doubts and weaknesses behind a façade of
wordiness and self-protective conformity. His very vulnerability is
a kind of strength.

A Passage to India:
Analysis and Revaluation

by Gertrude M. White

A Passage to India, apparently the last, and certainly the best of E. M. Forster's novels, was published twenty-nine years ago, in 1924. It was accorded instant recognition, as a fine novel and as a perceptive and sympathetic treatment of the problem of "Anglo-India." The years that followed saw the book established as a modern classic. It has reached a wide audience in the Everyman, Modern Library, and Penguin editions, and has challenged as well the attention of able critics. But, though the novel has received its just dues in many ways, there remains one aspect—and, I think, a fundamental one— still unexplored. It is acknowledged on all sides that thought is the most important element in Forster's novels;[1] yet the dialectical pattern of *A Passage to India* has never, to my knowledge, been fully and specifically recognized. This omission has resulted not only in a certain incompleteness in critical accounts of the book, but in not a little confusion and obscurity as well.

A score or more of penetrating studies have analyzed *A Passage* as a social document: "a book which no student of the Indian question can disregard."[2] Its plot, style, character-drawing, particular ideas

---

"A Passage to India: *Analysis and Revaluation*" by Gertrude M. White. From *PMLA 68 (1953): 641–57. Reprinted by permission of the Modern Language Association.*

[1] This point has been made by virtually every critic who has written on Forster. See specifically the following studies: E. K. Brown, "Revival of E. M. Forster," *Yale Review*, N.S. XXXIII (June 1944), 668–681; Virginia Woolf, "The Novels of E. M. Forster," *Atlantic Monthly*, CXL (Nov. 1927), 642–648; Lord David Cecil, "E. M. Forster," *Atlantic Monthly*, CLXXXIII (Jan. 1949), 60–65; Morton D. Zabel, "E. M. Forster," *The Nation*, CXLVII (22 Oct. 1938), 413–416; Rex Warner, *E. M. Forster* (London: Supplement to *British Book News*, 1950); et al.

[2] Peter Burra, "The Novels of E. M. Forster," *The Nineteenth Century and After*, CXVI (Nov. 1934), 583.

and attitudes have likewise been exhaustively discussed, evaluated, and related to the body of Forster's work and to modern literature generally. Its author has been hailed as "the last survivor of a cultured liberal tradition" (Warner, p. 5) and "the only living novelist who can be read again and again." [3]

Even those who have written of him with most appreciation, however, have apparently failed to grasp fully the meaning and importance of the novel's theme, and thus have given only partial accounts of it. Penetrating and provocative as they are, such treatments as those of Burra,[4] Trilling, Brown,[5] Zabel, and Hoare[6]—to name a few of the best—still tend to be over-general, and to put a somewhat undue emphasis on the "mystery" of the novel. Burra seems to speak for all of them when he tells us that its "thought, like music's, cannot be fixed, nor its meaning defined" (pp. 586–587). Though this is, no doubt, true in a sense, I feel that the mistiness of the book has been exaggerated.

This same failure to apprehend clearly the framework of thought in the novel has led other critics into undue censure or misunderstanding. For example, we hear that, "He beats the bush with admirable dexterity, but nothing appears. No wonder his book leaves on our minds an impression of waste." [7] Or we are told, "In his comedy . . . he shows himself the born novelist; but he aims also at making a poetic communication about life, and here he is, by contrast, almost unbelievably crude and weak." [8] These are severe judgments indeed.

[3] Lionel Trilling, *E. M. Forster* (London, 1944), p. 9.

[4] Pp. 581–594. This article was later reprinted as the introduction to the Everyman edition of *A Passage to India* (London, 1942), pp. xi–xxvii. Forster himself has praised it very highly.

[5] E. K. Brown, "E. M. Forster and the Contemplative Novel," *Univ. of Toronto Quart.*, III (April 1934), 349–361.

[6] Dorothy M. Hoare, "E. M. Forster," *Some Studies in the Modern Novel* (London, 1938), pp. 68–97.

[7] Ranjee G. Shahani, "Some British I Admire," *Asiatic Rev.*, XLII (July 1946), 273.

[8] F. R. Leavis, "E. M. Forster," *Scrutiny*, VII (Sept. 1938), 185. This article offers a perfect illustration of the misunderstanding into which even a competent critic may be led by a neglect of the novel's pattern of thought. Mr. Leavis selects, for a criticism of Forster's style, the paragraph in Chapter XXVI which describes the reactions of Fielding and Hamidullah to the news of Mrs. Moore's death, directing particular attention to the "lapse in taste" responsible for the final phrase of the sentence: "How indeed is it possible for one human being to be sorry for all the sadness that meets him on the face of the earth, for the pain that is endured not only by men, but by animals and plants, and perhaps by the stones?" This is what he says: "Once one's critical notice has fastened on it . . . can one do anything but reflect how extraordinary it is that so fine a writer should be able,

And there are those who openly confess themselves at a loss: "One can re-read a dozen times and be no nearer a solution." [9]

Any attentive reader of *A Passage* has certainly realized that Forster indeed suggests more than can be explained; and to translate suggestive and poetic language into explicit statement is always to risk destroying one kind of reality without furnishing another. It is my belief, however, that there exists in *A Passage* a dialectical pattern, strong and subtle, by which the author attempts to bind social, psychological, and philosophical levels into a harmony and to relate the characters and events of the novel to each other and to the informing idea of the whole. Further, I believe that incompleteness and misunderstanding alike can best be avoided by a grasp of this design, and that a clear understanding of it will contribute materially to a revaluation of the novel. It is my purpose in this paper to analyze the basic thought of the book as closely as possible. But an acknowledgment and a warning is first of all in order.

"To summarize any good, developed idea is to betray it" (Trilling, p. 51). It cannot be too strongly emphasized that the *schema* of the novel that follows is not the novel itself, which, in richness and complexity, far transcends it. The importance of *A Passage* lies in the way Forster has given life and force to the philosophical pattern, and they are right who seek its chief meaning in character, idea, attitude, and atmosphere: in all the multitudinous richness of texture and substance which the book offers. My excuse must be, not that the theme is the *major* thing in the book, but that it is the *basic* thing; and that its neglect causes even the most gifted reader to fail, at least partially, in appreciation and understanding.

It is generally agreed that Forster is a writer of the "contemplative" novel; and further, that all his novels tend to be illustrations of a single idea. This single theme is, in the critics' various terms, "the chasm between the world of actions and the world of being" (Brown,

---

in such a place, to be so little certain just how serious he is? For surely that run-out of the sentence cannot be justified in terms of the dramatic mood Mr. Forster is offering to render?" (pp. 198–199). An understanding of the novel's thought and peculiar method makes it clear, on the contrary, that this phrase is one more echo in a book of echoes; as will be obvious to anyone who troubles to read carefully the account of Godbole's vision of Mrs. Moore, the wasp, and the stone in the final section of the novel. What Mr. Leavis describes as a fault in style is, in terms of thought, mood, and structure, a conscious, deliberate, and effective device.

[9] E. B. C. Jones, "E. M. Forster and Virginia Woolf," *The English Novelists,* ed, Derek Verschoyle (London, 1936), p. 262.

UTQ, p. 352); "the search for the *wholeness* of truth," and the harmonizing of "the tragic antitheses of mankind" (Zabel, pp. 413, 416); the antithesis "between Real and not-Real, true and false, being and not-being." [10] Each book develops this single theme in somewhat different terms, and on many levels. The dominant idea of *A Passage* is best expressed by the Whitman poem from which the novel takes its title:

Passage to India!
Lo, soul, sees't thou not God's purpose from the first?
The earth to be spanned, connected by network,
The races, neighbors, to marry and be given in marriage,
The oceans to be crossed, the distant brought near,
The lands to be welded together.

Then not your deeds only O voyagers, O scientists and inventors, shall be
    justified,
All these hearts as of fretted children shall be soothed,
All affection shall be fully responded to, the secret shall be told,
All these separations and gaps shall be taken up and hook'd and link'd to-
    gether,
The whole earth, this cold, impassive, voiceless earth, shall be completely
    justified,

Nature and Man shall be disjoined and diffused no more,
The true son of God shall absolutely fuse them.

(O pensive soul of me—O thirst unsatisfied—waitest not there?
Waitest not haply for us somewhere there the Comrade perfect?)[11]

It is the theme of fission and fusion; of separateness and of desired union. The threefold division of the book, "Mosque," "Caves," and "Temple," which Forster himself tells us represent the divisions of the Indian year, the Cold Weather, the Hot Weather, and the Rains,[12] represent also a kind of Hegelian Thesis—Antithesis—Synthesis; or, more properly perhaps, the statement of the problem, and two opposite resolutions.

In Part I, "Mosque," the central problem, "all these separations and gaps," is set up and explored on many different levels. The most obvious gap, at first, is that between Indian and English. Chandrapore

[10] Rose Macaulay, *The Writings of E. M. Forster* (New York, 1938), p. 10.

[11] *Leaves of Grass*, Incl. ed. (New York, 1924), pp. 343–351.

[12] "Author's Notes," *A Passage to India* (London: Everyman, 1942), p. xxxi.

is two towns, the native section and the English civil station, from which the town "appears to be a totally different place." [13] The separation is complete: the civil station "shares nothing with the city except the overarching sky" (p. 8), the first hint of a division more fundamental than any human differences. The universe itself is to be a protagonist in the drama of the many and the one.

But these broad divisions are themselves divided. India is not one but a hundred, of which Moslem and Hindu are only the most noticeable. India is a muddle; nothing embraces the whole of it; no one race or creed or person can sum it up or know all of it; nor are differences clear cut: "Nothing in India is identifiable, the mere asking of a question causes it to disappear or to merge in something else" (p. 86). India, in fact, is presented to us throughout as the very place of division; the unhappy continent where separations are felt more profoundly than in other places; and later we shall learn that Aziz's picnic fails "because he had challenged the spirit of the Indian earth, which tries to keep men in compartments" (p. 127).

If the continent and its conquered inhabitants are not united, neither are the conquerors. The English, in their club from which all Indians are excluded, are divided among themselves by the same barriers. Those who have been for some time in India are different in outlook from the newcomers, who have not yet retreated behind the defenses of tradition, race, caste, and position. Major official looks down upon minor official; wives of major officials look down upon their inferior sisters. The soldier's attitude differs from the civilian's. And though the English woman does not live in purdah, as does the Indian lady, there is an antagonism between the sexes which raises a more subtle but as effective barrier between them: the women think their men "weak" in dealing with natives; the men believe, in their secret hearts, that it is their women who complicate matters.

The gaps and separations between human beings are not the only ones. Men themselves are separate from the rest of creation. Young Mr. Sorley, a missionary with advanced ideas, sees no reason why the mercy of God should not embrace all mammals; but he becomes uneasy if the conversation descends to wasps, and is totally unable to admit into the Divine unity "oranges, cactuses, crystals, and mud" (p. 38). Yet men are only a small part of creation: "It matters so little to the majority of living beings what the minority, that calls itself human, desires or decides" (p. 114). And the universe itself,

---

[13] *A Passage to India* (New York: Modern Library, 1940), p. 8. All future page references to the novel are to this edition.

powerful, indifferent, is apart from or even hostile to the concerns of all sentient creatures.

If multiplicity is the fact, unity of some sort is the desire. Separated from each other by race, caste, religion, sex, age, occupation, and the hundred barriers of life, men still must strive to unite with each other and to achieve some harmonious resolution of their differences. And they desire as well, though some of them may not know it, to find that unity that shall embrace the whole scheme of things, from which nothing shall be excluded. "Mosque" is therefore not only a symphony of differences but of attempts at oneness. But this unity which is sought is of two different kinds, which must be carefully distinguished. One is the unity of negation, the other of affirmation; one of exclusion, the other of inclusion. The one emphasizes differences and separations; the other reconciles them in a larger synthesis. The one merely breeds misunderstanding, violence, and hatred; the other seeks peaceful resolution.

The first, of course, is the more easily come by. The Indians are united among themselves only by hatred and suspicion of the English, the one force strong enough to bind together the different races and creeds. Within separate groups, such as Moslem and Hindu, they are united by their traditions, their history, their religion, and their art. Aziz and his friends, quoting the poetry of Islam, feel that India is one and their own; Aziz, visiting his mosque, finds the home of his spirit in that faith. And these forces, which bind together members of the same group, by the same token set them apart from those of other groups. Aziz, embracing a Hindu friend, thinks, "I wish they did not remind me of cowdung," at the same moment that his friend is thinking, "Some Moslems are very violent" (p. 267). The English, too, find the unity of exclusion, of suspicion, and of hatred. The anthem of the Army of Occupation reminds every member of the club that he is British and in exile, enabling them for the moment to sink their personal prejudices. Unity of this kind is achieved not *with* but *against;* it is essentially hostile and evil in nature, and the breeder of more hostility and more evil.

As the first kind of oneness affirms and ratifies the differences and separations natural to life, the second attempts to embrace and to reconcile them by good will, sympathy, kindness, and love. The effort may be on either a purely secular level, or on a religious basis. Fielding, the "holy man minus the holiness" (p. 121), believes that the world "is a globe of men who are trying to reach one another and can best do so by the help of good will plus culture and intelligence"

(p. 62). Adela desires to "see the real India" (p. 24); to learn and to understand. But though she has true good-will, she is deficient in emotional response; in "the secret understanding of the heart" (p. 20). From this deficiency all her future troubles will stem. Mrs. Moore, on the other hand, a Christian mystic, is made up of intuitive understanding and sympathy, of an all-embracing charity. It is she who reminds her son Ronny of the necessity for love in all relationships, the political as well as the personal; that God is Love.

In this first section, every event, every character, every detail is a variation on the same theme. The gulf between English and Indians is shown from both points of view: at the dinner in Hamidullah's home, in the English club, at the farcical "Bridge Party." But what a different story when Aziz, the Indian, meets the newcomers, who wish to communicate, to bridge the gap, who offer genuine good-will, kindness, even love. Instantly he responds to Mrs. Moore's understanding on their meeting in the mosque; instantly he makes friends with Fielding; he accepts, though he does not really like, Adela; and generously and at infinite pains he makes plans for the visit of the ladies to the Marabar Caves.

At the end of the section, it seems that brotherhood is about to triumph. The omens are auspicious: East and West have met and embraced; friendship and love are in the ascendant. Islam, whose symbol the mosque gives the section its title, preaches the eternal oneness of God. Christianity, the religion of the English, teaches the oneness of all men in the Divine love. The season of the year is the Cold Weather, most suitable to human life and activity; the climate in which men can live and grow. But "April, herald of horrors" (p. 115) is at hand: the Hot Weather, dangerous and oppressive to all life. Professor Godbole, the Hindu, has sung his haunting song of invitation to Shri Krishna, Lord of the Universe: "Come, come, come, come, come, come" (p. 80). But the god refuses to come. And his refusal poses the problem for the next section.

If Part I has been Thesis, the problem of separation and attempts at bridging the gulfs, Part II is Antithesis; for in "Caves" we see the utter rout of the forces of reconciliation, the complete triumph of hostility, evil, and negation.

The central episode of this section, and of the entire novel, is the experience of the two Englishwomen, Adela Quested and Mrs. Moore, in the Marabar Caves. It is a shattering experience, calamitous to everyone: it destroys Mrs. Moore both spiritually and physically;

it drives Adela to the brink of madness; it threatens ruin to Aziz, and actually alters his entire future; it imperils all relations between English and Indians; and it destroys all constructive relationships between individuals. Yet it is never satisfactorily explained by the author. The nature and meaning of Adela's and Mrs. Moore's experience is left in darkness, dealt with only in highly oblique and allusive language. What was the voice of the Marabar?

The Marabar Caves are the very voice of that union which is the opposite of divine; the voice of evil and negation; of that universe which is "older than all spirit" (p. 124). They are the voice of Chaos and Old Night, when "the earth was without form, and void, and darkness was upon the face of the deep"; long before the Spirit of God moved upon the waters and said, "Let there be Light." The answer they give to the problem of oneness is an answer of horror and despair, whether on the human or on the universal level.

To each lady, the voice of the Marabar speaks of a kind of oneness, but in different terms; terms appropriate to character, age, and situation. To the elder, the religious mystic who wishes to communicate with God, to become one with the universe, in the conviction that such union is beautiful and full of meaning, the echo speaks of a universe in which all differences have been annihilated, an infinity of Nothing. Good and evil are identical: "Everything exists, nothing has value" (p. 149). All has become one; but the one is Nothing. Here is unity with a vengeance! To the younger Adela, who has wished to understand but not to love India and the Indians, who has become engaged to a man she does not love, who is not convinced that love is necessary to a successful union, the meaning of the echo presents itself in different terms. To her, it speaks of the last horror of union by force and fear, without love. She believes that Aziz has attempted to assault her, goes nearly mad with horror, and sets in motion the machinery that shall prosecute and punish him. For the Marabar has revealed to her what such union is: Rape.

Upon Mrs. Moore, who had told her son that God is Love, the effect of the Marabar is immediate and profound despair. We have had hints of India's impact upon her previously. "God . . . had been constantly in her thoughts since she entered India, though oddly enough he satisfied her less. She must needs pronounce his name frequently, as the greatest she knew, yet she had never found it less efficacious. Outside the arch there seemed always an arch, beyond the remotest echo a silence" (p. 52). Since Professor Godbole had sung his queer song at Fielding's tea party, she had been apathetic. Already disillusionment is upon her, a sense of the futility of all attempts at union. "She felt increasingly (vision or nightmare?) that, though people are important, the relations between them are not, and that in particular too much fuss has been made over marriage; centuries of carnal embracement, yet man is no nearer to understanding man. And today she felt this with such force that it seemed itself a relationship, itself a person who was trying to take hold of her hand" (p. 135).

In this state of mind she enters the Marabar, and hears the echo of that oneness which is nothingness. "The mood of the last two months took definite form at last, and she realized that she didn't want to write to her children, didn't want to communicate with anyone, not even with God" (p. 150). From this moment, she takes no more interest in anything. She dismisses Adela's experience: "all this rubbish about love, love in a church, love in a cave, as if there is the least difference" (p. 202). Knowing Aziz to be innocent, she neither speaks nor stays to testify at his trial. She departs, in this season of the Hot Weather when travel is dangerous, and dies at sea. The echo has ended everything for her. To the Christian mystic the Marabar has said that the universe is muddle rather than mystery; the answer to its riddle is Nothingness.

To Adela the meaning of the echo has presented itself in terms very different, though nearly as disastrous. The keynote of her character, from the beginning, has been an honest but arid intellectualism. Unlike Mrs. Moore, with her intuitive sympathies and responses, Adela approaches the problems of life by means of the rational intellect. Her good will, her kindness, come not from the heart but from the head. Fielding is to point out to her that she fails because she has no real affection for Aziz or for Indians generally; she herself confesses to him that her instincts never help her.

Adela's engagement to Ronny has taken place only because of the accident to the Nawab Bahadur's car. Previously, she has refused to marry him; but the accident has linked her to him in a spurious union. The same forces that unite the English against outsiders have united the young man and woman. She does not love him; but until the day of the expedition this question has not even occurred to her. But now, as she goes with Aziz alone to explore a cave, she thinks for the first time, "What about love?" (p. 152), a question in some way suggested to her by a pattern in the rock similar to that traced in the dust by the wheels of the Nawab Bahadur's car. For the first time, she realizes that she and Ronny do not love each other.

"The discovery had come so suddenly that she felt like a mountaineer whose rope had broken. Not to love the man one's going to marry! Not to find it out till this moment! Not even to have asked oneself the question until now! . . . There was esteem and animal contact at dusk, but the emotion that links them was absent" (p. 152).

But Adela, being the person she was, "wasn't convinced that love is necessary to a successful union" (p. 152). Recovering herself, she drives Aziz from her side in embarrassment by her question, "Have you one wife or more than one?" and goes alone into the cave, there to undergo the ordeal, as she thinks, of his attempted rape.

The analogy here between the personal situation of Adela and Ronny, and the political situation between India and England is clear. It is almost as if she has felt about their personal relationship what Ronny feels about the union of India and England politically. He had told his mother that the English were not in India to be pleasant but "to hold this wretched country by force" (p. 50). Mrs. Moore had thought at that time that, "One touch of regret—not the canny substitute but the true regret from the heart—would have made him a different man, and the British Empire a different institution" (p. 51). The English are, for the most part, honest, sincere, incorruptible, earnestly attempting to do justice in administering India. But, as Mrs. Moore reminds her son. "Though I speak with the tongues of men and angels, and have not love . . ." (p. 52), it profits nothing. Aziz, in his illness, has told Fielding that what India needs is "Kindness, more kindness, and even after that more kindness. I assure you it is the only hope. . . . We can't build up India except on what we feel" (p. 117). Instead, the English are holding India by fear and force, without kindness or love. "Mosque" has been full of this sort of union: hostile, evil, and negative. Now Adela, joined to Ronny without love, by the same forces which operate to link together the English in India against native and outsider, experiences symbolically the utmost degradation of such union.

The effect of their experience in the Marabar is to quench every little flame of kindness and good will in those around them. The bridges thrown across the gulfs crumble; the abysses widen and deepen. Evil and negative unity alone is left. The English draw together more firmly than ever against natives, in a union that annihilates all reason, all justice, and all mercy. Fear and hate unite the Indians in Aziz's defense. Fielding, throwing in his lot with them, realizes at that moment the profundity of the gulf that divides him from them. The evil spreads and propagates; the spirit of violence stalks abroad; the echo of the Marabar, spouting from its cave, has spread until it threatens to engulf the lives of everyone. Adela, recovering from her ordeal, is troubled by the echo, which still sounds in her ears. She feels in some vague way, contrary to what her intellect tells her, that she has committed a crime, is leaving the world worse than she found it. Attempting to understand what has happened, she is puzzled by the difference between what she *feels* and what she *knows*, and says incoherently, "I shouldn't mind if it had happened anywhere else; at least I really don't know where it did happen" (p. 199). For it has not happened to her, in the Marabar; it has happened everywhere in India, it has happened in all places and at all times when men attempted union without love.

Mrs. Moore, engulfed in her own failure and her own despair, refuses help. Nevertheless, her mere presence helps Adela's echo, and suggests the possibility of a mistake. The machinery she has set in motion grinds on; and after Mrs. Moore's departure, though the question of an error still occurs to her intellect, it ceases to trouble her conscience. But at the trial, it is the name of Mrs. Moore, chanted like an incantation by Indians who do not know what the syllables mean, that shows Adela the truth, as in a vision: that nothing "in reality" had happened to her in the Marabar. The charge is withdrawn and Aziz saved. Adela's echo vanishes. Aziz, consulting Mrs. Moore's spirit, renounces the compensation that would have ruined his enemy. And Fielding and Adela, attempting to understand the whole muddle, have to give it up. "She was at the end of her spiritual tether, and so was he. . . . Perhaps life is a mystery, not a muddle; they could not tell. Perhaps the hundred Indias which fuss and squabble so tiresomely are one, and the universe they mirror is one. They had not the apparatus for judging" (p. 263).

Though the spirit of Mrs. Moore has averted the ultimate disaster, nothing good is left: the Marabar has brought nothing but evil. Political relationships have been imperilled; personal ones fare no better. Adela is rejected by the English community; Ronny breaks his engagement. Fielding, also cast out by his compatriots, is misunderstood by the Indians, his friendship with Aziz wrecked by the latter's suspicion of treachery. Kindness and good will have failed; of all the hopes and tentative gestures of union in Part 1, nothing is left but hatred, force, and fear. The Marabar has triumphed.

"Mosque," symbol of Islam; of human desire for that unity which is the indubitable attribute of God; of the Cold Weather, favorable to human lives and hopes: the problem in its multifarious forms. "Caves" is one answer; the voice of chaos, of a universe of evil and annihilation, and of the Hot Weather, that climate in which men cannot live. But the caves are only one part of India. As Mrs. Moore's ship sails from Bombay, "thousands of coco-nut palms appeared all round the anchorage and climbed the hills to wave her farewell. 'So you thought an echo was India; you took the Marabar caves as final?' they laughed. 'What have we in common with them, or they with Asirgarh?' " (p. 210). It may be that the voice of the chaos older than all spirit is not the final one. "Temple," title of the third section of the novel, is the symbol of the Hindu religion; of a possible reconciliation of differences not in negation but in a larger synthesis; of a universe which is perhaps a mystery rather than a muddle, a riddle to which an answer exists; and of the Rains, token of renewed life, of regeneration, and of hope.

"Temple" opens with the enigmatic figure of the Hindu, Professor Godbole, who has appeared briefly in the first two sections. It is he who has invoked the god, at Fielding's tea party, in his song; he who has refused to answer Aziz's questions about the Marabar at that same time; and he with whom Fielding has had a curious and inconclusive conversation about good and evil at the time of the trial. Godbole, a Hindu mystic, is utterly immersed in the life of the spirit; so much so, indeed, as to be completely unfitted for practical action or decision. He dwells entirely in the world of being, and men of action, like the English generally and Fielding in particular after the Marabar expedition, find him maddening.

Godbole thus represents in his person the life of the spirit developed to its uttermost degree: he stands at the opposite pole from Ronny and the English in general, who excel at the practical life but are lost in the spiritual. Philosophically, he stands for that universality characteristic of Hinduism. Unlike Islam and Christianity, Hinduism makes no distinctions between humanity and the rest of the creation; its creed teaches that each particular part is a member of all other parts, and that all is one in the Divine. In his talk with Fielding, Godbole expresses the belief that nothing can be performed in isolation; that all perform a good action when one is performed, and when an evil action is performed, all perform it. Evil and good alike express the whole of the universe. Further, good and evil are both aspects of God. He is present in the one, absent in the other. "Yet absence implies presence, absence is not non-existence, and we are therefore entitled to repeat, 'Come, come, come, come'" (p. 178). Godbole, then, stands for the union in reality of all men, whether they will or no, and for a universe in which God exists, though he may at a particular time and place not be present; for a universe which may be a mystery but is not a muddle.

In the festival which opens the "Temple" section, the celebration of the birth of Shri Krishna, universality is the theme. At the birth of the god, "all sorrow was annihilated, not only for Indians, but for foreigners, birds, caves, railways, and the stars; all became joy, all laughter; there had never been disease nor doubt, misunderstanding, cruelty, fear" (pp. 287–288). The voice of the Marabar is drowned in this festival, in which "Infinite Love took upon itself the form of Shri Krishna, and saved the world" (p. 287). And Godbole, developing the life of his spirit, in a vision sees Mrs. Moore, united in his mind with a wasp seen he forgot where: an echo of an earlier discussion on the all-embracing mercy of God.

It is a prophetic vision, for what happens in "Temple" is reconciliation on the human level, the cancelling of the effects of the Marabar. Reconciliation, not real union; that is not possible on earth, whatever may be the truth about that universe of which earth is only an atom. The hundred voices of India say, "No, not yet," and the sky says, "No, not there" (p. 322). But the most painful human differences are soothed: Aziz and Fielding resume their friendship, though it can lead no further; Aziz finally makes his peace with Adela.

These things are brought about by Mrs. Moore, who returns to India in the guise of her children, Stella, whom Fielding has married, and Ralph, son of her flesh and still more of her spirit. It is the spirit of love, of intuitive understanding, which triumphs at last, in spite of her personal defeat. She had herself told Ronny, "I think everyone fails, but there are so many kinds of failure" (p. 52). Hers had been a failure of *understanding*, but not of *love*. Her memory, and the presence of her son, Ralph, completely change Aziz's attitude from hostility to homage: "He knew with his heart that this was Mrs. Moore's son, and indeed until his heart was involved he knew nothing" (p. 313). And at Mau, too, Fielding and Stella are brought close together: "There seemed a link between them at last—that link outside either participant that is necessary to every relationship. In the language of theology, their union had been blessed" (p. 318). The Marabar has been wiped out.

"All invitations must proceed from heaven perhaps; perhaps it is futile for men to initiate their own unity, they do but widen the gulfs between them by the attempt" (p. 37). So Forster seems to be saying. *A Passage to India* is a novel of these gulfs, of the bridges thrown across them, of the tensions that hamper and threaten communication, of the failure and the horror of all efforts at union without love, and of whether Oneness when found is Something or Nothing. Since it is a great novel, it is, of course, far more than its dialectical pattern. But a grasp of that pattern in its full detail enables us to evaluate the novel more fully and fairly than has yet been done, and to arrive at an estimate of its author's achievement. We can now appraise Forster's apparently final effort to incarnate his difficult ideas; we can ask whether he has given them satisfactory aesthetic form, has success-fully solved the problem which, as a novelist, he has set himself.

A Passage to India is not, as some critics have claimed, an expres-sion of Forster's personal disillusion. Nor is it "almost unbelievably crude and weak" in its attempt at making a poetic communication about life. It is the last and best of Forster's attempts in that most difficult genre, the novel of ideas. It is an almost-successful attempt at an all-but-impossible task: an attempt to fuse the real world of social comedy and human conflict with the meaning and value of the uni-verse which that world mirrors; to impose on experience the pattern of a moral vision; and out of these disparate elements to create a satisfying aesthetic whole. The wonder is not that it fails of complete success, but that it so nearly succeeds completely.

In *A Passage* appear the recurrent themes, the characteristic at-titudes, and the peculiar gifts displayed by its author in his earlier fiction, integrated fully at last into the novel's structure and ex-pressed in its characters, episodes, and atmosphere. Forster has found in it a thesis and a medium that enable him to use his full strength and to minimize or conceal his weaknesses. It is at once the finest and the most typical of his books, revealing most clearly his individual quality and distinction.

This is not to deny that, in some measure, the book is a failure. All good critics of Forster have remarked, in their different ways, upon the "double vision" apparent in his books: the contrast and often collision between the realistic and the symbolic, the two levels upon which characters and events exist and function. The most serious charge that has been laid at his door is that he is unable "to create realistic form, credible form, moving form" (Brown, *YR,* pp. 668–681); that his characters are inadequate to the ideas they in-carnate; that his preoccupation with these ideas "leads him outside the limits of consciousness that his comedy would seem to involve"

(Leavis, p. 185); that, in the words of Virginia Woolf, one of his most
friendly critics, "his difficulty is to persuade his different gifts to
combine into a single vision" (p. 643). He is both poet and satirist,
both comedian and moralist, both preacher and artist. A mocking
spirit of fantasy flouts his reality, poetry ruffles his prim surface, and
his books, instead of being artistic wholes, are racked and rent by
interior disharmony, the result of the tensions between his ill-assorted
gifts and his contradictory aims.

From this charge, *A Passage* cannot wholly be absolved. Mr. Trilling, in his full-length study of Forster, has remarked upon the imbalance of its plot to its story. Its characters, he tells us, are right for
the plot but not large enough for the story. By "story" Trilling seems
to mean the thought I have just analyzed: the dialectical pattern of
the book. The plot, as distinguished from this larger theme, is the
story of Aziz; the tale of what goes on in his mind in the course of
his tragically unsuccessful attempt to overcome the "separations and
gaps" which divide him from Mrs. Moore and Adela. We see him
progress from almost total ignorance to complete awareness of the
unjust situation in which he is placed, and for which, as he comes to
see, there is no remedy in human action. He retreats from Chandrapore to Mau, from the English and their Western science to a
remote jungle where he can "let his instruments rust, [run] his little
hospital at half steam, and [cause] no undue alarm" (p. 290). His
failure and his disillusionment, humanly speaking, are the real center
of interest in the novel.

Yet Aziz, however imaginatively realized as a man and an Indian,
is, as Mr. Trilling observes, not large enough for the "story": for the
cosmic stage on which his adventures are played. Though he comes
to realize the uselessness of attempts at friendship and union, he
never apprehends the real significance of his own ordeal nor relates it to
the ordeal of India and of the whole world. Not for him, any more
than for Ronny, Adela, or Fielding, is the world outside the arch,
the silence beyond the echo. "It is useless discussing Hindus with me,"
he tells his friend during their last ride together. "Living with them
teaches me no more" (p. 320).

On the other hand, the two "redemptive" characters large enough
for the cosmic stage move among their human companions awkwardly,
not wholly at ease with the world and the flesh. Mrs. Moore and
Godbole are never really satisfactory as human beings, never vitally
related to the people and events around them. Their human features
are veiled by the larger-than-life masks they wear, like the actors in
Greek tragedy playing at being gods. We perceive their effect with-

out understanding or really accepting it; we take them at the valuation assigned by their author, but we do not put our own valuation
upon them nor stamp them with the seal of our affirmation.

Thus, the gulf between symbol and reality, so often noticed in
Forster's work, is again the chief feature, and in a sense, the chief
failure of *A Passage to India*. The author tries hard to bridge it; but
he does not quite succeed. Those who read the book as social comedy,
or as an analysis of the Indian question, though they will find much
to enjoy and admire, will be baffled and irritated again and again by
the suggestion of a meaning far deeper than appears. To them,
Godbole will be a nuisance, Mrs. Moore incomprehensible, Adela's
adventure in the Marabar cave mere hysteria, and the Temple section
irrelevant and incoherent. And those who perceive the larger "story,"
the immense and mysterious context into which the human adventures
of Aziz and Adela are fitted, will also perceive more poignantly the
crack between comic manner and cosmic meaning. "Between the conception / And the creation / Between the emotion / And the response / Falls the Shadow." The shadow of the double vision falls
upon *A Passage,* as it does upon the earlier books: the real and the
symbolic worlds co-exist independently instead of blending into one
another and becoming a whole.

But only in this ultimate sense does the book fail. In all else it
triumphs. Humor and poetry, those unlikely companions, walk arm
in arm: tenderness and deep insight offer their balm to the sharp
sting of satire. We have heard these themes—we have perceived these
attitudes—we have met these people—we have watched these scenes—
we have savored this delicate and lyric prose in Forster's earlier books.
But we have never seen theme and character and attitude so clear,
so free of ambiguity and doubt, we have never seen comedy so deft
and light-handed, poetry so poignant. Not as a frieze but as a spirit,
Anglo-India, India herself, pass before us. Their hundred voices sound
in our ears, their pains and perplexities become our own and those
of the whole world.

The value of personal relationships, the holiness of the heart's affections, always important in Forster's novels, is central to the theme,
the characters, and the episodes of *A Passage*. Error and evil are the
inevitable consequences of the failure of love between human beings:
of the disastrous personal failure of Adela, and the no less disastrous
social and political failure of the English officials and their wives.
And whatever is saved from the wreck—Aziz's life, Adela's reason,
Fielding's and Aziz's friendship—is saved by love alone: the love
represented by Mrs. Moore's spirit. Whatever the level, human or

divine, love is the only salvation. "Kindness, more kindness, and even after that more kindness. I assure you it is the only hope." This theme is the dominant note of *A Passage,* the keystone of its structural arch.

In the same way, in that "suspicion of action and of beliefs which sometimes seems to amount to passivity and defeatism" [14] which has been noted as characteristic of Forster, he is here leading from strength rather than weakness. For he here creates a world in which, whether it be on the social, the political, or the philosophical plane, sharply defined beliefs and active policies are productive of nothing but tension, hatred, strife, and disunion. Definite beliefs, Christian, Moslem, or Hindu, English or Indian, do but divide men more sharply from each other; and the world of action is the nightmare world of the English club, the Indian riot, the courtroom, the "world of telegrams and anger" shown at its most hostile and destructive. Neither beliefs nor action can save us, Forster says, and in *A Passage* compels us to believe, but only "the secret understanding of the heart," which may fail but can never be really defeated, and is our only answer to the voice of the Marabar.

So too Forster's dissatisfaction with civilization, with that humane and liberal culture which produced him and which he represents is, in *A Passage,* integrated into the plan of the book in a more vital sense than was true of the earlier novels. Did Margaret Schlegel really marry Henry Wilcox? We have never quite believed it. But we can believe in Fielding, in his effort and in his failure, for we see —how clearly!—what Fielding is up against, and we see too that his cultivated agnostic spirit is wholly unable to comprehend the awful mystery or muddle of the world beyond the arch. Fielding believes in good will plus culture and intelligence; but we see him baffled and wistful before the dim apprehension of something, he knows not what—something his wife knows and Mrs. Moore had known. *A Passage* shows, far more fully and satisfactorily than Forster's earlier books, the inadequacy, the collapse, of the liberal-bourgeois-agnostic mind face to face with the ultimate mystery at the heart of the universe. The hollowness of Margaret Schlegel's world stands for the first time fully revealed.

Even one of Forster's real weaknesses as a novelist, his "demurely bloodless gaiety," [14] that embarrassment before the sexual relation which mars his other novels without exception, is a source almost of

[14] "Morton D. Zabel, 'A Forster Revival'" (review of Trilling), *The Nation,* CLVII (7 Aug. 1943), 158–159.

strength in *A Passage.* For his task here is not to portray a pair of lovers, and to fail at making them lovers, as was true, for example, of George and Lucy in *A Room With a View.* His intention is to show us a young man and woman who attempt to become lovers and who are temperamentally unequipped for their rôles. So, while it may be said that Ronny and Adela are one of the least attractive pairs in fiction, it may also be said that it is necessary to the purpose and effect of *A Passage* that this should be so. They are not there to show love and the life of the senses triumphant, as George and Lucy were—and to fail, as George and Lucy failed—but to show the horror and disaster of attempts at union *without* love.

The same thing is true of Forster's gifts of character-drawing, of social satire, and of that lyrical sensibility so oddly contrasted with it. A few deft strokes, and the English ladies—Mrs. Turton, Mrs. Callendar, Mrs. McBryde—are forever impaled in all their shallow and insular arrogance. Fielding, the holy man minus the holiness, is both more sympathetic and more vivid than his prototype, old Mr. Emerson. The portraits of the Indians, Hamidullah, the Nawab Bahadur, Mahmoud Ali, Mr. Das, form a varied gallery of individuals who never degenerate into types, and are crowned with that triumph of insight and imaginative sympathy, the figure of Aziz: most interesting, most human, most believable of all Forster's characters. Satirist of the collision between the English middle class and an alien culture, Forster creates in *A Passage* some unforgettable scenes: the discussions at the English club; the trial; the Indian riot; both comedy and satire given sharper edge and more pungent acidity by the deceptive lightness and grace of touch. And the poet who describes the Marabar caves, or the festival of Shri Krishna, evokes for us the very spirit of the Indian earth and conveys a sense of the ineluctable mystery of human existence.

It is true, as E. K. Brown has reminded us, that the end of fiction is the realistic representation of life, and that a novel is not saved by a great theme (*YR*, pp. 668–681). But a novel which displays such gifts of political penetration and social comedy, such beauty of language and depth of character-portrayal, is not rendered less great by a theme that is worthy of it, and which it manages so very nearly to subdue into a complete aesthetic pattern. In defiance of all modern canons of criticism, I believe it is sometimes preferable to fail of complete success in a great venture than to succeed wholly in a petty one; and by that token, I believe with Brown that *A Passage to India* is and will remain "the subtlest effort in our time to write the novel of ideas in English."

Passage To and From India

by Nirad C. Chaudhuri

Reading *A Passage to India* some time ago, I was led to think not only of the final collective passage of the British from India but also of Mr. Forster's contribution to that finale. Such an association of ideas between a novel and an event of political history may be objected to, but in this case I think the association is legitimate. For *A Passage to India* has possibly been an even greater influence in British imperial politics than in English literature.

From the first, the more active reaction to it followed the existing lines of political cleavage, its admirers being liberal, radical, or leftist sheep and its detractors conservative, imperialist, and diehard goats. The feud between English liberalism and the British empire in India was as old as the empire itself. Except for a short period of quiescence when Liberal-Imperialism was in vogue, it raged till 1947. Mr. Forster's novel became a powerful weapon in the hands of the anti-imperialists, and was made to contribute its share to the disappearance of British rule in India.

On those, also, who did not follow clear party cues in respect of India, its influence was destructive. It alienated their sympathy from the Indian empire. As it was, the British people taken in the mass were never deeply involved in this empire, emotionally or intellectually. To them it was rather a marginal fact of British history than what it really was—a major phenomenon in the history of world civilisation. Mr. Forster's book not only strengthened the indifference, it also created a positive aversion to the empire by its unattractive picture of India and Anglo-Indian life and its depiction of Indo-British relations as being of a kind that were bound to outrage the English sense of decency and fair play. Thus, the novel helped the growth of that mood which enabled the British people to leave

"Passage To and From India" by Nirad C. Chaudhuri. From Encounter *2 (June 1954): 19–24. Reprinted by permission of* Encounter.

India with an almost Pilate-like gesture of washing their hands of a disagreeable affair.

Even intrinsically, the novel had a political drift. There is of course no necessary connection between a writer's own intentions and the manner in which he is accepted or exploited by his public. It has even been said that it is only when they are debased or deformed that philosophical ideas play a part in history. But in regard to *A Passage to India*, it can be said that the author's purpose and the public response more or less coincided. The novel was quite openly a satire on the British official in India. Perhaps in a veiled form it was also a satire on the Indians who were, or aspired to be, the *clientes* of the foreign patriciate. As such it was, at one remove, a verdict on British rule in India. At the risk of depriving it of its nuances, but perhaps not misrepresenting its general purport, I might sum it up as follows. This rule is the cause of such painful maladjustment in simple human relations that even without going deeply into the rights and wrongs of the case it is desirable to put an end to it. The intention seems to have been to bring even English readers to agree with the last outburst of the hero of the novel, Aziz: "We shall drive every blasted Englishman into the sea, and then you and I shall be friends."

Accordingly, one is almost forced to appraise the novel as a political essay on Indo-British relations, and as soon as it is considered as such, a striking gap in Mr. Forster's presentation of these relations fixes attention. It is seen that the novel wholly ignores the largest area of Indo-British relations and is taken up with a relatively small sector. The ignored area is the one I watched at first hand from the age of seven to the age of fifty. The other sector, in contrast, was known to me only by hearsay, because I feared its contact almost as much as a Pharisee feared the contact of publicans and sinners.

The Indo-British relations I was familiar with were contained, for the most part, within the conflict between Indian nationalists and the British administration. Here I saw great suffering and distress, but also exultation, a brave acceptance of ill-treatment and conquest of weak tears. The longer the men had been in jail, the more they had been persecuted, the more "sporting" they seemed to be. In the other sector, the conflict was between associates, the British officials and their Indian subordinates or hangers-on, and had all the meanness of a family quarrel. It sizzled without providing any ennobling or even chastening release for passion, only distilling rancour. It con-

tributed much to the pathology of Indo-British relations but virtually
nothing to the final parting of ways. If we can at all speak of having
driven the "blasted Englishman into the sea," as Aziz puts it, it was
not men of his type who accomplished the feat. Those who fought
British rule in India did not do so with the object of eventually
gaining the Englishman's personal friendship. Just as personal hu-
miliation did not bring them into the conflict, personal friendship
did not also lure them as a goal.

But of course there was good reason for Mr. Forster's choice. The
reason is not however that the political conflict was impersonal and
could not be treated in a novel. It could be, though the result would
have been a tragedy of mutual repulsion and not a tragi-comedy of
mutual attraction. Mr. Forster chose the sector of which he had personal knowledge. As an Englishman paying a short visit to India, he
naturally saw far less of Indians in general than of his own country-
men and of the Indians with whom the latter had official business or
perfunctory social relations. Being an Englishman, of humane sen-
sibilities, he was also shocked by the state of these relations, as among
others Wilfrid Blunt was before him. On the other hand, he could
not observe the larger and the more important area without going
considerably out of his way and making a special effort.

There is also another and not less fundamental reason for Mr.
Forster's choice. That is the character of his political consciousness. I
should really call it humanitarian consciousness. For his is an appeal
in a political case to the court of humane feelings to what he himself
calls "common humanity" in a later essay. Now, the relationship between common humanity and politics is even more complex than
that which exists between morality and politics. I firmly believe that
ultimately, politics and morals are inseparable; even so, the most
obvious moral judgement on a political situation is not necessarily a
right judgement, and for humane feelings to go for a straight tilt at
politics is even more quixotic than tilting at windmills.

The consequences of pitting humane feelings against a political
phenomenon are well illustrated in *A Passage to India*. One consequence is that it leads to pure negation. In the sphere of Indo-British
relations the novel has no solution to offer except a dissolution of
the relationship, which is not a solution of the problem but only its
elimination. The good feeling that such a dissolution can generate,
and has in actual fact generated between Indians and the British
after 1947, is the sort of kindly feeling one has for strangers or casual
acquaintances. It is of no use whatever for a sane ordering of political

relations which one is struggling to raise from an amoral or even immoral level to a moral one.

Another consequence is that the humanitarian prepossession leads Mr. Forster to waste his politico-ethical emotion on persons who do not deserve it. Both the groups of characters in *A Passage to India* are insignificant and despicable. I have, however, my doubts about Mr. Forster's delineation of his countrymen. I am no authority on the life of White officials in India, for I never cultivated them. Still, observing them in their public capacity, and at times laying incredible stupidities at their door, I did not consider them quite so absurd a class as Mr. Forster shows them to be.

Of one implied charge I will definitely acquit them. Mr. Forster makes the British officials of Chandrapore nervous about the excitement of the Muharram to the extent of making the women and children take shelter in the club, and after the trial of Aziz he makes them reach home along by-ways for fear of being manhandled by a town rabble. Of this kind of cowardice no British official in India was to my mind ever guilty, even in their worst time since the Mutiny, in the years 1930 to 1932, when the Auxiliary Force armoury at Chittagong in Bengal was raided by a band of young revolutionaries, British officials were shot dead in Calcutta and the districts, and attempts were made on the life of the Governor of Bengal and the Police Commissioner of Calcutta. As a class, the British officials kept their head. The courage shown by the District Magistrate of Chittagong on the night of the raid, when an insurrection of unknown magnitude and danger faced him, was admirable. The shortcoming of the British official was not in courage, but in intelligence.

On the other hand, Mr. Forster is too charitable with the Indians. Aziz would not have been allowed to cross my threshold, not to speak of being taken as an equal. Men of his type are a pest even in free India. Some have acquired a crude idea of gracious living or have merely been caught by the lure of snobbism, and are always trying to gain importance by sneaking into the company of those to whom this way of living is natural. Another group of men are more hard-boiled. They are always out to put personal friendship to worldly profit, perhaps the most widespread canker in Indian social life even now. Indian ministers and high officials feel this even more strongly than Ronny in Mr. Forster's novel. These attempts at exploitation are making them more outrageously rude than any British official, and all the more so because in India there is no tradition of kindliness among people in power. In British days this bickering gave rise to a corrosive race conflict, now it is fomenting an equally corrosive class conflict. But it is futile to grow censorious over this, no sane or satisfactory human relations can be built up with such material.

Mr. Forster appears to have felt this himself. He is too intelligent to be able to overlook the weak points in the Indian character, and too honest to suppress them in his book. Indeed, he shows himself so acute in seizing them that it is impossible to imagine that he was representing Aziz and his associates as fine fellows who deserved to be treated as equals by the British, and was not conscious of their utter worthlessness. I detect a personal admission in the comment he puts in the mouth of Ronny about the Nawab Bahadur, the "show Indian": "Incredible, aren't they, even the best of them?" So I am not surprised to find a streak of satire even in his presentation of Indians. But such satire not being his aim, he is driven into a corner, from where he can plead for satisfactory Indo-British relations on the only basis which could be proof against disillusionment, the basis of the least respect and the largest charity. Inevitably he has also to make a moralist's impossible demand on human nature.

But even if Mr. Forster's Indians had been good as individuals as they are malodorous, he would not have had a very much stronger case. For he had not chosen his Indian types happily. In regard to the Hindu characters, he relied mostly on the types found in the Princely States. Certainly they were more traditional than those in British India, but they were so traditional that they did not represent modern India at all. For instance, to those of us who are familiar with the teachings of the Hindu reformers of the 19th century, Godbole is not an exponent of Hinduism, he is a clown. Even for us, friendly personal relations with these men became possible only if we assumed we were in an anthropological reserve. Although the States have now been incorporated in India, the unevenness persists, and it presents a serious problem of *Gleichschaltung* for the future.

But Mr. Forster's more serious mistake was in taking Muslims as the principal characters in a novel dealing with Indo-British relations. They should never have been the second party to the relationship in the novel, because ever since the nationalist movement got into its stride the Muslims were playing a curiously equivocal role, realistic and effective politically, but unsatisfying in every other respect. The Muslims hated the British with a hatred even more vitriolic than the Hindu's, because it was they who had been deprived of an empire by the British. Yet they found themselves wooed by the latter as a counterpoise to the Hindu nationalists, and they did not reject these overtures.

They were shrewd in their calculations. They knew that their own battle was being fought by the Hindus and that in an eventual victory their share of the spoils was guaranteed. In the meanwhile, it was profitable to exploit the British, make the best of both worlds. This game, played with boldness and hardheaded realism, succeeded beyond expectation and created an independent state for the Muslims of India.

But a colossal Machiavellian game of politics like this could be played without moral risks only by men of very great strength of character, as indeed all the Muslim leaders, from Sir Sayyid Ahmad Khan to M. A. Jinnah, were. On the rank and file of the Muslims, so far as this policy influenced them, it had a deplorable effect. It left one section unweaned from its barren and rancorous hatred and made another pine for British patronage. Aziz and his friends belong to the servile section and are all inverted toadies. With such material, a searching history of the Muslim destiny in India could have been written, but not a novel on Indo-British relations, for which it was essential to have a Hindu protagonist.

But I think I know why Mr. Forster would not have a Hindu. He shares the liking the British in India had for the Muslim, and the corresponding dislike for the Hindu. This was a curious psychological paradox and in every way unnatural, if not perverse. On the one hand, the Islamic order was the natural enemy of the Christian-European, and the British empire in India was in one sense the product of the secular conflict between the Christian West and the Islamic Middle East, which is still running its course. More than one British Foreign Secretary found the pitch of British policy queered by the incurable phil-Islamic attitude of the British Indian Government, and once Sir Edward Grey expressed frank annoyance at it.

On the other hand, there was between European civilisation and the Hindu in its stricter form a common Indo-European element, which was discovered and described by British Orientalists in the first century or so of British rule, but which came to be forgotten and ignored by Englishmen in later times. Modern Hindu thinkers did not, however, lose sight of the affinity. Swami Vivekananda, speaking at the end of the last century, said that two branches of the same people placed in different surroundings in Greece and India had worked out the problems of life, each in its own particular way, but that through the agency of the British people the ancient Greek was meeting the ancient Hindu on Indian soil, and thus "slowly and silently the leaven has come, the broadening out, the life-giving revivalist movement that we see all around us." The British in India never gave this fruitful idea any encouragement. They were taken in by the deceptive simplicity of the Muslim and repelled by the apparent bizarrerie of Hinduism and its rococo excrescences. I wonder if it was the Hebraic element in the British ethos which was responsible for this.

This leads me straight to my objections to the politics of *A Passage to India* and my one positive comment on its central theme. My most serious criticisms are the following. It shows a great imperial system at its worst, not as diabolically evil but as drab and asinine; the rulers and the ruled alike are depicted at their smallest, the snobbery and pettiness of the one matching the imbecility and rancour of the other. Our suffering under British rule, on which a book as noble as Alfred de Vigny's *Servitude et grandeur militaires* could have been written, is deprived of all dignity. Our mental life as depicted in the book is painfully childish and querulous. Lastly, attention is diverted away from those Indians who stood aloof from the world the book describes and were aristocratic in their way, although possessing no outward attribute of aristocracy. When I consider all this I feel Mr. Forster's literary ability, which has given the book its political importance, as a grievance.

At the root of all this lies the book's tacit but confident assumption that Indo-British relations presented a problem of personal behaviour and could be tackled on the personal plane. They did not and could not. The great Indians who brought about the Westernisation of their country and created its modern culture had none of the characteristic Indian foibles for which Mr. Forster invokes British compassion. They were men of the stature of an Erasmus, Comenius, or Holberg, who could hold their own with the best in Europe. Yet some of them were assaulted, some insulted, and others slighted by the local British. None of them had any intimate personal relations with any member of the British ruling community. There were also thousands of Indians who had adopted Western ideals and were following them to the best of their ability, who were not only not cultivated but shunned with blatant ostentation by the British in India. "What you have got to stamp on is these educated classes," they all said, like the subaltern in the novel. This was due, not to any personal snobbery, but to that massive national snobbery which refused to share British and Western civilisation with Indians.

Those who remember the powerful championship of Westernisation by Macaulay usually forget that his best supporters were Indians and his most determined opponents his own countrymen. In spite of the formal adoption of this policy, the British ruling class in India never felt happy about it and carried it out halfheartedly. Towards the result, the attitude of the thoughtful Englishman was one of regret, while the average Englishman grew maliciously quizzical.

To give only one example, there was hardly one Englishman who had a good word to say about our employment of the English language. I still remember the pleasure I felt when for the first time in my experience, I read praise of our English in Sir Michael Sadler's report on Calcutta University. Normally the better our English the more angry did the Englishman become, and the worse it was the greater was the entertainment of the Memsahib and *ergo* the larger the favours of the Sahib. Even so great a personage as Lady Minto was not above the weakness, and in his kindly manner even Mr. Forster has felt amused by our English.

Of course, I cannot deny that much of our English as indeed much of our Westernisation was quaint. But ours were the shortcomings of self-taught and unguided men everywhere. If, in their days of power, the British had not looked askance at our employment of English, today the battle for English in India would not have been already lost, and we should not have needed the forlorn crusade of the British Council, too late for love, too late for joy, too late, too late!

Once the premise of cultural apartheid was admitted, there could be no advance on the personal plane, for men do not treat as equals those who are not of their psychological species. The British in India clinging to the obsolete idea of zoological speciation for mankind, could only cry as the District Collector does in *A Passage to India*: "I have never known anything but disaster result when English people and Indians attempt to be intimate socially. Intercourse, yes. Courtesy by all means. Intimacy—never, never."

A real Englishman, greater than Mr. Forster's Turton, had come to the same conclusion. Sir Edwin Lutyens, the builder of New Delhi, tried friendship with Indians and wrote in disenchantment: "The natives do not improve on acquaintance. Their very low intellects spoil much and I do not think it is possible for the Indians and Whites to mix freely and naturally. They are very different, and even my ultrawide sympathy with them cannot admit them on the same plane as myself. They may be on a higher plane or a lower one than a White, but the ethics of their planes are different to ours, and for one or the other to leave his plane is unclean and unforgivable."

On the other hand, putting the cultural impact in the foreground, Indians propounded a strikingly contrasted thesis. At that level our personal humiliations ceased to matter and even our great *injuria temporum*, political subjection, presented a second face. Rammohun Roy was grossly insulted by a British baronet and official. He protested against it to the Governor-General but did not allow it to influence his views on Westernisation or even those about British rule in India. He surprised a young French scientist, Victor Jacquemont, who saw him in Calcutta, by an expression of opinion which the Frenchman set down verbatim in his journal: *"La conquête est bien rarement un mal, quand le peuple conquérant est plus civilisé que le peuple conquis, parce qu'elle apporte à celui-ci les biens de la civilisation. Il faut à l'Inde bien des années de domination anglaise pour qu'elle puisse ne pas perdre beaucoup en ressaisissant son indépendance politique."*

Bankim Chandra Chatterji, the creator of Hindu nationalism, was actually assaulted by a British official though a magistrate himself, but he too, when it came to assessing the larger consequences of British rule in India, argued persuasively that it was in many ways providential. Personal grievance, even when well-founded, did not influence men of this type.

The contrast between the generosity of such Indians and the British narrowness furnishes the key to the real failure of the British in India. It was the failure to see that a nation which was not willing to propagate its civilisation and extend its spiritual citizenship was also incapable of perpetuating, not only an empire, but even friendly political relations with other nations not belonging to its own culture complex. The challenge before the British was to create an open society in the order of the mind. Their opportunity was to make India an extension of the Western world. But they failed as completely in using their opportunity as they did in meeting the challenge. Compared with this failure, which was a betrayal of the West in India, their bad manners were mere peccadillos.

This political evaluation of *A Passage to India* has not been attempted for its historical interest, great as that interest is. I believe that the questions which British rule raised in India have only been put aside and not answered by what happened in 1947. I also believe that the British failure to understand the true nature of the Indo-British relationship has a moral, whose application is likely to widen as time passes, for a new set of international relations taking shape today over an area very much larger than India. It is this moral that I have to draw now.

But as a preliminary I should define my position. I represent no school of thought in India, past or present, and there is nothing characteristically Indian in my views except the fact that they are those of an Indian by birth and are based on Indian experience. I differ fundamentally from the nationalistic majority of my country-men who speak of 19th century imperialism but forget that the century also had its nationalism. I differ no less fundamentally from the influential minority in India who believe in world government, who pin their faith to a world government of the contractual type, carried on by means of a world assembly in which the national repre-sentatives will be wise, reasonable, and just. I cannot say, like a Christian, that this conception is bound to be wrecked on the innate sinfulness of man, but I would say that it would hurtle against man's inherent urge to power.

It seems to me that the West is now showing the same incompre-hension which destroyed British power in India. The economic and the political impact of the West is being felt. What is absent is that proselytising cultural impact which alone can counteract the mental resistance to the extension of Western culture into the non-Western parts of the world. Instead, there is the same uncritical faith in the promotion of economic prosperity and the converting power of *Pecunia Americana* as there was in the maintenance of law and order and the indispensability of *Pax Britannica*. The West ought to, and in my opinion can, think in terms of something higher than effective diplomacy, higher even than world government, for converting the single zoological species called man into one psychological species. Of course, that might not be possible. But one can never speak of impossibility before an effort has been made.

A Passage to India

by Frederick C. Crews

. . . Is the novel, then, a covert apology for Hinduism? Many readers have thought so, but at the expense of oversimplifying Forster's attitude. Hinduism is certainly the religion most able to cope with the bewildering contradictions one finds in India, but its method of doing this—accepting everything indiscriminately, obliterating all distinctions—has obvious disadvantages that are brought out in the course of the novel. The tripartite structure of *A Passage to India*, with its formal shifting from "Mosque" to "Caves" to "Temple," suggests that various religious paths to truth are being problematically offered; and the inconclusive and frustrating ending of the book implies that each path, while having particular advantages that the others lack, ultimately ends in a maze.

Those who favor a Hindu reading of *A Passage to India* rest their claims on the final section of the novel, where the setting has changed from Westernized Chandrapore to a Hindu Native State. In these surroundings there is, indeed, occasion for a meeting of East and West. But the meeting, which takes place at the peak of the Hindu festival of Gokul Ashtami, is effected through the capsizing of two boats in a furious rainstorm, and it is a moot question whether the momentarily reconciled parties have been drenched with Hindu love or simply drenched. It is a climax, Forster warns, only "as far as India admits of one" (p. 315), and in retrospect the festival amounts only to "ragged edges of religion . . . unsatisfactory and undramatic

Extracts from E. M. Forster: The Perils of Humanism *by Frederick C. Crews* (Princeton: Princeton University Press, 1962; London: Oxford University Press, 1962), pp. 151–63, 178–80. Copyright © 1962 by Princeton University Press. Reprinted by permission of the publishers. The footnotes have been renumbered. The editions quoted from are as follows: A Passage to India, 1924; Two Cheers for Democracy, 1951; Abinger Harvest, 1936; Aspects of the Novel, 1927 (all published in New York by Harcourt, Brace & World, Inc.); and Howards End, New York, 1954.

tangles." (p. 316) If Hinduism succeeds, where Islam and Christianity fail, in taking the entire universe into its view, we still cannot silence the voice of Western humanism. What about man and his need for order? Are we to sacrifice our notion of selfhood to the ideal of inclusiveness? "The fact is," Forster has said elsewhere, "we can only love what we know personally." (*Two Cheers*, p. 45) And as Fielding thinks when he has quit India and recovered his sense of proportion at Venice, "Without form, how can there be beauty?" (p. 282)

These misgivings about reading *A Passage to India* in a spirit of orthodoxy are strengthened by an acquaintance with Forster's private statements of opinion about the religions involved. We know, of course, that such statements cannot take the place of internal evidence, but in this case the internal evidence is somewhat ambiguous; the temptation to ask Forster what he really thinks is irresistible. His attitude toward Christianity is hardly obscure, but Islam and Hinduism have aroused mixed feelings in him, and these, I think, find their way into *A Passage to India*. On his second trip to India, in 1921, Forster was Private Secretary to the Maharajah of Dewas State Senior, a Hindu Native State; his letters from there and elsewhere are sometimes revealing. "I do like Islam," he wrote to his mother from Chhatarpur, "though I have had to come through Hinduism to discover it. After all the mess and profusion and confusion of Gokul Ashtami, where nothing ever stopped or need ever have begun, it was like standing on a mountain." [1]

The nature of this attraction is evident in two essays reprinted in *Abinger Harvest*, "Salute to the Orient!" and "The Mosque." Islamic meditation, Forster explains, "though it has the intensity and aloofness of mysticism, never leads to abandonment of personality. The Self is precious, because God, who created it, is Himself a personality. . . ." (*Abinger Harvest*, p. 273) One thinks immediately of Forster's well-known individualism; the idea of selfhood is indispensable to his entire system of value. Again, Forster's liberalism and his contempt for superstition seem to govern the following contrasts between Islam and Christianity: "Equality before God—so doubtfully proclaimed by Christianity—lies at the very root of Islam . . ." and the Moslem God "was never incarnate and left no cradles, coats, handkerchiefs or nails on earth to stimulate and complicate devotion." (*Ibid.*, pp. 275, 276) Nowhere does Forster imply that he actually believes the dogmatic content of Islam; the point is that he is aes-

[1] *The Hill of Devi* (New York, 1953), p. 193.

thetically gratified by a religion that is not grossly anthropomorphic. He is no more of a Moslem than he is a Christian, but Islam at least does not outrage his common sense and his love of modest form.

A Passage to India, of course, demands more of religion than this; the central question of the novel is that of man's relationship to God, and Moslems, Forster says, "do not seek to be God or even to see Him." (*Ibid.,* p. 273) Thus Islam can hardly lead Forster's characters to the assurance they need; as Fielding puts it, " 'There is no God but God' doesn't carry us far through the complexities of matter and spirit; it is only a game with words, really, a religious pun, not a religious truth." (*A Passage to India,* p. 276) And the refusal to abandon personality, which is the strongest bond between Aziz and the Westerners in the novel, turns out to be a severe limitation in their apparatus for grasping transcendent truth.

Forster's opinion of Hinduism is more clearly a dual one: he finds Hindu ritual absurd but Hindu theology relatively attractive. His letters about Gokul Ashtami are extremely condescending; he thought the spirit of the festival indistinguishable from "ordinary mundane intoxication," and he generalized: "What troubles me is that every detail, almost without exception, is fatuous and in bad taste." [2] Yet his admiration for the Maharajah for whom he was later to work led him to an early sympathy with Hindu doctrine. The following excerpt from a letter of March 6, 1913 explains part of the Maharajah's position and Forster's response to it:

"His attitude was very difficult for a Westerner. He believes that we—men, birds, everything—are part of God, and that men have developed more than birds because they have come nearer to realising this.

"That isn't so difficult; but when I asked why we had any of us ever been severed from God, he explained it by God becoming unconscious that we were parts of him, owing to his energy at some time being concentrated elsewhere. . . . Salvation, then, is the thrill we feel when God again becomes conscious of us, and all our life we must train our perceptions so that we may be capable of feeling when the time comes.

"I think I see what lies at the back of this—if you believe that the universe was God's *conscious* creation, you are faced with the fact that he has consciously created suffering and sin, and this the Indian refuses to believe. 'We were either put here intentionally or unin-

[2] *The Hill of Devi,* pp. 160, 159.

tentionally,' said the Rajah, 'and it raises fewer difficulties if we suppose that it was unintentionally.' " [3]

Here again we may observe that Forster is not asserting a religious belief of his own, but is simply trying to be openminded. Still, we can recognize the congeniality of Hinduism, in this interpretation, to Forster's opinions as we already know them. His disbelief in Providence, his sense of man's ignorance of divine truth, his rejection of the idea of a man-centered universe—all are reconcilable with his summary of the Maharajah's Hinduism. Yet the point at which the correspondence breaks down is even more striking. It is easy enough for Forster to entertain the theory that God is presently unconscious of man, but there is little provision in his philosophy for the moment of awakening; only the negative side of Hinduism accords with his temperament.

There is no escaping the impression that Hinduism is treated with considerable sympathy in *A Passage to India*. Its chief function, however, seems to be to discredit the Christian and Moslem emphasis on personality; the vastness and confusion of India are unsuitable for an orderly, benevolent deity whose attention to individuals is tireless. When the question of mystical union arises, however, Forster becomes evasive in the extreme. Gokul Ashtami, he remarks, presents "emblems of passage; a passage not easy, not now, not here, not to be apprehended except when it is unattainable. . . ." (*A Passage to India*, pp. 314f.) Although Hinduism offers the most engaging fable to describe our isolation from meaning, it, too, like Islam and Christianity, seems powerless before the nihilistic message of the Marabar Caves.

The incidents in the Caves are of course the symbolic heart of the novel, where India exerts its force of illusion and disillusion upon the British visitors. These incidents are meaningful on all levels, making the hopeless misunderstanding between East and West vivid and complete, but their most important kind of meaning is clearly religious. The Christian Mrs. Moore and the Moslem Aziz, having befriended one another in a mosque, have previously been kept apart by social barriers, but now they are to meet, with Adela, on the ground of what Adela has called "the real India." The Marabar Caves will offer them an India more virginal than they bargain for, and will, through utter indifference to selfhood, challenge their very sense of reality.

[3] *ibid.*, p. 45.

The Marabar Hills, "older than all spirit," date back to an age long before Hinduism arrived and "scratched and plastered a few rocks." (p. 124) They are "flesh of the sun's flesh," and the sun "may still discern in their outline forms that were his before our globe was torn from his bosom." (p. 123) They are thus completely divorced from the works and history of man. Like the Hindu God, they seem to have no attributes: "Nothing, nothing attaches to them," says Forster. (p. 124) And this analogy with Hinduism is highly suggestive, for Mrs. Moore's experience in the Hills is a kind of parody of the recognition of Brahma. Hinduism claims that Self and Not-self, Atman and Brahman, are actually one, and that the highest experience is to perceive this annihilation of value. Value is indeed annihilated for Mrs. Moore; the echoing Caves convince her that "Everything exists, nothing has value." (p. 149)

Glen O. Allen has found several references in the *Upanishads* to the dwelling of Atman and Brahman in caves,[4] and one such passage seems especially pertinent here. "The wise who, by means of meditation on his Self, recognises the Ancient, who is difficult to be seen, who has entered into the dark, who is hidden in the cave, who dwells in the abyss, as God, he indeed leaves joy and sorrow far behind." [5] In the Marabar Caves Mrs. Moore discovers "the ancient," but it is not Brahma: "What had spoken to her in that scoured-out cavity of the granite? What dwelt in the first of the caves? Something very old and very small. Before time, it was before space also. Something snub-nosed, incapable of generosity—the undying worm itself." (p. 208) And though she does, indeed, leave joy and sorrow behind, the departure is utterly pedestrian. She has simply been thrust into the disillusion of old age: "She had come to that state where the horror of the universe and its smallness are both visible at the same time—the twilight of the double vision in which so many elderly people are involved. If this world is not to our taste, well, at all events there is Heaven, Hell, Annihilation—one or other of those large things, that huge scenic background of stars, fires, blue or black air. All heroic endeavor, and all that is known as art, assumes that there is such a background . . . But in the twilight of the double vision, a spiritual muddledom is set up for which no high-sounding words can be found; we can neither act nor refrain from action, we can neither ignore nor respect Infinity." (pp. 207f.)

[4] Glen O. Allen, "Structure, Symbol, and Theme in E. M. Forster's *A Passage to India*," *PMLA*, LXX (December 1955), 934–954.

[5] *The Sacred Books of the East*, ed. F. Max Müller (Oxford, 1884), Vol. XV: *The Upanishads*, p. 10.

Readers who have claimed that Mrs. Moore has suddenly been transformed from a modest Christian to a mystical Brahmin have had to overlook the prosaic quality of her feelings here. She has had, in effect, an antivision, a realization that to see through the world of superficial appearances is to be left with nothing at all. "The abyss also may be petty, the serpent of eternity made of maggots. . . ." (p. 208)

Mrs. Moore's inversion of Hinduism is sharpened by the resemblance of the Caves' echoes—"boum" and "ou-boum"—to the mystic Hindu syllable "Om," which stands for the trinity of the godhead. He who ponders this syllable, says the *Prasna-Upanishad,* "learns to see the all-pervading, the Highest Person." [6] This is Mrs. Moore's ambition: "To be one with the universe! So dignified and simple." (p. 208) In an ironical sense she achieves this, for she does grasp a oneness underlying everything. Its monotony, however, is subversive of the moral and ceremonial distinctions that we require to reconcile ourselves to the Absolute. ". . . Religion appeared, poor little talkative Christianity, and she knew that all its divine words from 'Let there be Light' to 'It is finished' only amounted to 'boum.' " (p. 150) The oneness Mrs. Moore has found has obliterated her belief in the categories of space and time, distinctions that are essential to a religion whose God has a sense of history. This is why she can be said to have perceived both the horror and the smallness of the universe; the Marabar Caves "robbed infinity and eternity of their vastness, the only quality that accommodates them to mankind." (p. 150) . . .

We may well ask at this point why Mrs. Moore, who seems to have a kind of second sight on occasion and who is certainly a morally sympathetic character, is visited with disillusionment. One answer may simply be that she *does* have second sight, that she perceives what truly subsists behind the veil of Maya; in this case her experience would constitute a thorough disavowal of Hinduism on Forster's part. Remembering Adela's hallucination, however, we may question whether Mrs. Moore has penetrated anything at all. Perhaps she has merely heard echoes of her own unvoiced misgivings about the significance of life.[7] It is impossible, in any case, to support the

---

[6] Quoted by Allen, *PMLA,* LXX, 943.

[7] The Caves not only deliver a dull echo in reply to every sound, they also offer reflections of light on their polished walls. The flame of a match and its reflection, we are told, "approach and strive to unite, but cannot, because one of them breathes air, the other stone." (p. 125) In symbolic terms this seems to support

popular reading that she has experienced the merging of Atman and Brahman. Atman is the presence of the *universal* ego in the individual, the "God dwelling within," and the properly disciplined Hindu will find Brahman, the supreme soul, echoed in this "Self." Mrs. Moore, however, is unprepared to relinquish her selfhood in the narrow sense of personality. Instead of blending her identity with that of the world soul, she reduces the world-soul to the scale of her own wearied ego, her dilettantish yearning for oneness with the universe has been echoed, not answered. Whether or not Forster considers the serpent of eternity to be made of maggots is a question we cannot answer on the basis of *A Passage to India*; in view of his skepticism it is doubtful that he would feel himself qualified to make any assertion at all on the subject. What does emerge clearly from the novel is that the Marabar Caves have not brought us into the presence of ultimate truth. The last words of India to Mrs. Moore, as she sails away to die, may serve also as a caveat to eager critics: "So you thought an echo was India; you took the Marabar caves as final? . . . What have we in common with them, or they with Asirgarh? Good-bye!" (p. 210)

Adela's experience in the Cave, though it has religious implications, lends itself more readily to analysis in psychological terms. This agrees with the Caves' function of echoing only what is brought to them, for Adela's yearnings are sexual, not mystical. As she climbs upward with Aziz her conscious thoughts are occupied with her approaching marriage to Ronny, but she is increasingly troubled by misgivings, until she realizes with vexation that she is not in love with her fiancé. Before entering the Cave, however, she commits the Forsterian heresy of deciding that love is not essential to a successful marriage; she will marry Ronny anyway. As in the case of Mrs. Moore, the Marabar Caves thrust to the surface a conflict between conventional and suppressed feelings. The echo that is metaphorically sounded in Adela's hallucination (if it is a hallucination) of sexual attack is that of her unvoiced desire for physical love.

That this problematic assault should be attributed to Aziz is perhaps the central irony of plot in *A Passage to India*. Forster takes pains to let us know that Aziz's thoughts about sex are "hard and direct, though not brutal" (p. 102)—exactly the reverse of Adela's. Though he generally "upheld the proprieties . . . he did not invest

---

the idea that one will "see" his own thoughts imprisoned in Marabar stone, i.e. robbed of their context of human illusion.

them with any moral halo, and it was here that he chiefly differed from an Englishman." (p. 103) As for Adela, he finds her sexually repellent ("She has practically no breasts," he tells Fielding; p. 120), whereas Adela, for her part, is attracted to him ("What a handsome little Oriental he was . . ."; p. 152). Just before she enters the Cave, whose significance is apparently Freudian as well as metaphysical, Adela enviously ponders Aziz's physical advantages: "beauty, thick hair, a fine skin." (p. 153) She asks him, in what Forster calls "her honest, decent, inquisitive way: 'Have you one wife or more than one?' " (p. 153) And when the monogamous widower Aziz passes into a Cave to hide his embarrassment over her question, Adela enters a different Cave, "Thinking with half her mind 'sight-seeing bores me,' and wondering with the other half about marriage." (p. 153) It is this other half, this wondering about physical gratification, that accosts her in the Cave; and, since Self and Not-self are confused there, she assigns her thoughts to Aziz.

An important difference between Adela's crisis and Mrs. Moore's is that Mrs. Moore adjusts her whole view of life to accord with the annihilation of value in the Cave, while Adela continues for a while to be torn between accepting and rejecting her experience. Mrs. Moore knows intuitively that Aziz is not a rapist, but she is weary of legalistic distinctions; the alleged crime "presented itself to her as love: in a cave, in a church—Boum, it amounts to the same." (p. 208) She does not stay to testify for Aziz, for the moral issue of the trial cannot interest her; if there is no value in the universe, there is surely none in distinctions between sanctioned and illicit love. Yet this very indifference makes it proper that Mrs. Moore, after she has withered out of bodily existence, should be resurrected as a Hindu goddess in the minds of the Indians at Aziz's trial. "When all the ties of the heart are severed here on earth," says the *Katha-Upanishad*, "then the mortal becomes immortal. . . ." [8] The parallel is in one sense ironic, as we have seen: Mrs. Moore has been the victim of a travesty of Hindu enlightenment. On the other hand, the Mrs. Moore who originally befriended Aziz and who is remembered fondly by Professor Godbole has believed in loving everything that enters her consciousness, and such a love is the cornerstone of Hinduism.

Unlike Mrs. Moore, Adela lacks the imagination to be permanently shattered by her irrational experience. "In space things touch, in time

[8] *The Sacred Books of the East,* xv, 23.

things part" (p. 193), she repeats to herself, attempting to re-establish the categories that were imperilled by the Caves. Though she has been a freethinker, she turns to Jehovah for redress: "God who saves the King will surely support the police," goes her reasoning (p. 211). From the day of the hallucination until the climax of the trial she continually seeks to reconstruct the incident in direct logical terms. The dark savage has attacked her—but who has been the savage, Aziz or herself? Her virtue has been threatened—or has she simply rebelled against her starched prudery? Justice will be exacted upon the guilty one—but who is to cast the first stone in matters of sex? The psychological complexity of Adela's situation lends a kind of realistic support to Professor Godbole's doctrinal view: "All perform a good action, when one is performed, and when an evil action is performed, all perform it." (p. 177)

Forster would not assert this as a fixed principle, but we have often enough observed him recoiling from its opposite, the black-and-white attribution of guilt and innocence to separate parties. Before Adela can be freed from the echo of the Cave she must retreat a little from her simplistic Western notion of cause and effect. She is finally able to retract her charge because she has achieved a "double relation" to the controversial event: "Now she was of it and not of it at the same time. . . ." (p. 227) In other words, she has begun to feel the limitations of a knowledge that is strictly bounded by her personality, her discrete selfhood. If she is never to know what occurred in the Cave, at least she will remember that there may be an order of truth beyond the field of her rational vision. Like Fielding, whose empiricism has brought him no closer to knowledge than her own resort to prayer, Adela has reached "the end of her spiritual tether . . . Were there worlds beyond which they could never touch, or did all that is possible enter their consciousness? They could not tell. . . . Perhaps life is a mystery, not a muddle; they could not tell. Perhaps the hundred Indias which fuss and squabble so tiresomely are one, and the universe they mirror is one. They had not the apparatus for judging." (p. 263)

A Passage to India, then, is a novel in which two levels of truth, the human and the divine, are simultaneously explored, never very successfully. Epistemological conclusions are reached, but they are all negative ones. Christian righteousness, we discover, helps us to misconstrue both God and man; Moslem love can scarcely reach beyond the individual personality; rational skepticism is wilfully arid; and the Hindu ideal of oneness, though it does take notice of the totality of things, abolishes the intellectual sanity that makes life endurable to the Western mind. The inescapable point of this demonstration is that God cannot be realized in any satisfactory way. It is a point that Forster dwelt upon at some length in his earlier novels, but always with a note of smugness; there was always the facile warning that we should restrict our interest to the world that we know. In *A Passage to India*, however, Forster's characters are given no choice; if they are to understand themselves and one another they must grapple with metaphysics. They do their best, but it is very little—not because they are exceptionally weak, but simply because they are human. Forster implies that we ourselves, his readers, are equally blocked off from meaning. We cannot fall back on reason and the visible world, for we see how these are falsely colored by personality. Even if we could, we ought not seek Mrs. Moore's "dignified and simple" identification with the universe, for this is nihilism in disguise. Nor can we assert with humanistic piety that our whole duty is to love one another; this, too, proves more difficult than we might have gathered from Forster's previous books. What finally confronts us is an irreparable breach between man's powers and his needs.

It is perhaps significant that Forster's career as a novelist comes to an apparent end at this moment of development, for the characters of a novel, as he has said elsewhere, "suggest a more comprehensible and thus a more manageable human race; they give us the illusion of perspicacity and power." (*Aspects of the Novel*, p. 99) *A Passage to India*, though it tells us more about its characters than they themselves know, tries to refute the very thought that our race is comprehensible and manageable; it casts doubt upon the claim of anyone, even of the artist, to supply the full context of human action. In writing one novel which pays full deference to the unknown and the unknowable, Forster thus seems to announce the end of the traditional novel as he found it; between pathetic futility and absolute mystery no middle ground remains for significant action. . . .

. . . This book escapes the limitations of its predecessors because it has those limitations for its subject, and makes of them a solid masterpiece of pessimism.

A Passage to India thus strikes me as Forster's sole claim upon posterity. And yet the claim seems to be a substantial one. Since we have already studied this novel in detail, let us simply review its position in Forster's career. The progress of his art, we might say, is a movement from commentary about behavior (moral questions) to statements about reality (existential questions). The two Italian novels, with their rather simple ethical dilemmas and their formal infliction of comic justice upon the unworthy characters, are almost exclusively moral; the metaphysical views of Mr. Emerson, for example, are not tested out but are simply intruded into the narrower issue of Lucy's emancipation from "society." Already in *The Longest Journey*, however, we find that the *meaning* of Rickie Elliot's existence nearly overshadows the moral question of what he should do with his life. Indeed, Rickie's moral choices gain their significance only from an elaborated background of theories about the size, uniformity, and ethical character of the universe; and the clash of these theories, while parallel to the crisis of the plot, begins to assume an independent interest. In *Howards End* this metaphysical preoccupation is continued: Margaret Schlegel cannot control her life until she has widened her sense of truth. But it is precisely to the degree that Forster is seriously pursuing the question of existence that his novel seems forced and brittle; for, as we have seen, his instinctive sense of reality is hostile to the chins-up resolution of his plot. When Forster proclaims hopefully at the end, "Let Squalor be turned into Tragedy" (*Howards End*, p. 330), he is trying to rescue the novel from its own metaphysics—from the conclusion that the human order of meaning is of very small consequence to the universe at large.

Hence the necessity, fulfilled in *A Passage to India*, of a novel that passes beyond humanistic morality to a basically metaphysical critique of man's fate. Forster's last novel, unlike the others, refuses to suggest that we can be saved or damned through our behavior; its main point is that God's will, if it exists at all, cannot be known in human terms. I believe that *A Passage to India* is a great book, not because it takes this line of argument—a bad novel, after all, could have been written in the same spirit—but because in drawing upon Forster's profoundest feelings and building itself around them with bold consistency, it achieves aesthetic freedom. Here at last Forster accepts with his whole imagination the destructive ironies of his humanism, rather than stifling them with ambiguous claims about "hope even on this side of the grave." (*Howards End*, p. 103) The result is a novel whose resources of plot and symbolism work in harmony toward a single end, and whose subdued prose reverberates, like the voice of Mrs. Moore, to swell the night's uneasiness. Forster's theme is now sufficiently grand, and his relationship to it sufficiently controlled, for his novel to stand unsupported by moralizing rhetoric. Ironic understatement, which has always been his most effective manner, is here set free to bring all human endeavor into a single focus of description and evaluation.

I should insist, finally, that this triumph of self-criticism does not constitute a betrayal of the liberal humanism that pervades the earlier novels. The essence of that humanism, as it is expressed in the "coinage" chapter of *The Longest Journey,* is a pessimistic awareness of the disparity between human meaning and supernatural truth: a sense not only of the futility of otherworldliness, but of the instability of earthly value. The humanist is portrayed from the first as the owner of a paralyzing knowledge of man's limitations, a seeker after truth who knows that he is ill-equipped to make sense of the world. *A Passage to India* makes us feel the pathos of this condition more vividly than its predecessors, for it refuses to glamorize the relatively slight reassurance that is left to the humanist when he has turned his back on heaven. The original picture, however, is not essentially changed. Forster's last novel merely emphasizes more vividly the impossibility—except perhaps in art—of victory over fortune and time. Humanistic tolerance and sympathy remain the cardinal Forsterian virtues, but they lead to no splendid reward and must simply be exercised in the absence of any better way of getting along.

If *A Passage to India* is, as I believe, incomparably superior to the rest of Forster's fiction, it is nevertheless not a tour de force. It is, rather, the culminating expression of Forster's refinement of liberalism. Like *The Magic Mountain,* also published in 1924, it expresses the self-scrutiny of a mind that is anchored in liberalism and yet aware of weaknesses in the liberal tradition. Like Mann, Forster rests his masterpiece on a foundation of intellectual integrity; his nearly suicidal eclecticism becomes a weapon for aesthetic victory over the partiality and error it reveals. The victory belongs to reason, but to reason defining the limits of reason. We could see in such novels, if we wished, the formal surrender of liberalism to the self-doubts that have always tormented it; but we may see them equally as announcing the severance of liberal ideals from the narrow dogmas of progress and profit. Forster's career as a novelist, in any case, finally brings him away from the fashionable slogans of sexual equality, self-expression, and even social responsibility, and places him briefly in the company of those great writers who have looked steadily, with humor and compassion, at the permanent ironies of the human condition.

E. M. Forster's Island

by C. B. Cox

In his last two novels Forster tries hard to deal with the sources of power in society, the Wilcoxes and the Anglo-Indian officials, but he is repeatedly guilty of superficiality. Evie and Charles Wilcox are both caricatures, treated with no sympathy. If we place George Eliot's Bulstrode by the side of Charles, we can see how little Forster understands. His reaction to will-power and energy is one of emotional disgust; and there is a basic fastidiousness in both his style and his attitudes to people. Large parts of the masculine world are nauseous to him. He mocks athletics, in the person of Gerald in *The Longest Journey,* and satirizes the exercises practised by the Wilcoxes. And in the scene where Margaret has lunch with Herbert, this fastidiousness is even extended to hearty eating. "Saddles of mutton were being trundled up to expectant clergymen," he tells us, with a shudder of distaste.

In his treatment of the Anglo-Indians these emotions become violent and abusive. After the arrest of Aziz, the Collector becomes hysterical about the Indians: "You shall pay for this, you shall squeal . . . ," he thinks to himself; "he wanted to flog every native that he saw." And Mrs. Turton adds to this: "they ought to be spat at." These episodes, together with Fielding's rebuff at the club, are written with great force. We are shocked by the self-satisfied cruelty of the English middle classes. But the total effect never rivals in power the sense of evil evoked by writers such as Conrad or Faulkner. We are still too close to caricature and melodrama, and the conflict lacks tension as a result.

What we feel most strongly is Forster's disgust at those who try to rule. He is pandering to the liberal's instinctive dislike of adminis-

---

Extract from "E. M. Forster's Island," in The Free Spirit *by C. B. Cox (London: Oxford University Press, 1963), pp. 86–89. Copyright © Oxford University Press, 1963. Reprinted by permission of the publisher. The chapter from which this short extract is taken offers a penetrating critique of Forster's ethical assumptions.*

trators. The limitations of his own theories are seen particularly in his treatment of Heaslop. Our sympathies are directed towards Aziz, whose tenderness makes him "incapable of administration," and away from Heaslop, whose good sense is made to seem complacent and smug. Heaslop is honest and conscientious in his work as a magistrate; after the British have been successful in preventing bloodshed between Mohammedans and Hindus during preparations for the Mohurram procession, he feels pleased because his work is of some value, but immediately his self-satisfaction is mocked. The care for individual Indians, the attack on British complacency, the ideal of toleration, all are most successfully presented; but the effect of *A Passage to India* would be much greater if more justice were done to the Anglo-Indian sense of duty. Things aren't so jolly easy.

Forster's dislike of administrators is a product of his belief in freedom. No restrictions must be placed on individual liberty; if a man is tied down by the need to adapt himself to dogma or convention or to other people, he sacrifices some part of his essential human nature. This view of freedom, which has dominated much liberal humanist thinking of the last century, is based on an idealistic interpretation of reality. It leads Forster into muddle. For example, Fielding tries to travel light through life; he does not want to limit his freedom by becoming too closely involved with other people. But his friendship with Aziz makes him realize the difficulties in maintaining this position: "Travelling light is less easy as soon as affection is involved. . . ." If this is so, who wants to travel light? Forster confronts this problem when Fielding's sympathy drives him to take sides with Aziz before the trial. But Fielding is never satisfied to be so committed, and feels that there is something in him that restrains him from full participation in human relationships. The desire for freedom prevents him from achieving a full life.

That Forster would not accept this conclusion is seen in his treatment of marriage. *A Room With a View* ends with an ordinary marriage; but as George and Lucy on their honeymoon kneel together to look at the River Arno out of their hotel window, they have slipped away into the world of romance. There are many signs that Forster always thinks of love in this way. Fielding's love for his wife is a sudden joy which carries him through the marriage ceremony, but we see little of the companionship between mature people which ought to result. *The Longest Journey* includes some very odd views of marriage. Rickie is reproved for not keeping his wife "in line": "He had shown her all the workings of his soul, mistaking this for love;

and in consequence she was the worse woman after two years of marriage. . . ." Forster believes that few people are suited to travel the
long journey of life in close contact with each other:

> There are men and women—we know it from history—who have been
> born into the world for each other, and for no one else, who have ac-
> complished the longest journey locked in each other's arms. But romantic
> love is also the code of modern morals, and, for this reason, popular.
> Eternal union, eternal ownership—these are tempting baits for the
> average man.[1]

This passage reflects the cynicism of a hardened bachelor for lovers
"locked in each other's arms," and attacks the marriage contract.
According to Forster, this is rarely a mutual pledge and normally
satisfies only the desire for ownership. Like Shelley in *Epipsychidion,*
from which the title of the novel is taken, Forster cannot be satisfied
by the limitations imposed by marriage. And so the conclusion is
quite incredible. Stephen does not consult his wife when he decides
to take their child to sleep with them in the open, but treats her as
someone to be kept in line. What this means is not clear; the general
effect suggests a fear of complete committal to love and serve another
person.

   This distrust of marriage is further reflected in *A Passage to India.*
In her depressed condition after the incident in the Marabar Caves,
Mrs. Moore becomes bitterly cynical: "centuries of carnal embracement, yet man is no nearer to understanding man." This might be
ascribed to Mrs. Moore's breakdown, but that Forster has some
sympathy is shown by his treatment of Adela. When she gets engaged
to Heaslop, she feels dissatisfied. Previously she and Heaslop had
been unable to identify the creatures they saw during their walk at
the Maidan: ". . . unlike the green bird or the hairy animal, she was
labelled now . . . she felt humiliated again, for she deprecated
labels. . . ." She feels an instinctive dislike of committing herself to
a definite course of action; her freedom is limited, and she, together
with Forster, fails to see that such involvement, the relation of herself to other people and to societies, is a necessary part of a complete
life. After the trial is over, she and Fielding agree that love danger-
ously invades their private identity:

---

[1] [*The Longest Journey,* World's Classics, 1960], ch. xxxiii. p. 312.

"I no longer want love," he said . . .

"No more do I. My experiences here have cured me. But I want others to want it." [2]

The implication is that love is a dream, but that we pay too high a price for its romance by the sacrifice of our liberty. And so when Fielding eventually marries, Forster withdraws some of his sympathy from him. We are told that his faith in his educational work has grown more unrelenting since his income, with which he supports his wife, depends on it. He even doubts his own courage in the past:

> He had thrown in his lot with Anglo-India by marrying a country-woman, and he was acquiring some of its limitations, and already felt surprise at his own past heroism. Would he today defy all his own people for the sake of a stray Indian? [3]

That commitment leads to compromise on moral issues is inevitably true, and Forster is right to remind us of this. But he fails to recognize that his own ideal of travelling light is a denial of life.

[2] [*A Passage to India*, Everyman's Library, 1948], ch xxix. p. 228.
[3] Ibid., ch. xxxvii. p. 279.

Dogmatic Form

by Barbara Hardy

In *Aspects of the Novel* E. M. Forster has this to say about Hardy's novels:

> They are to be tragedies or tragi-comedies, they are to give out the sound of hammer-strokes as they proceed; in other words Hardy arranges the events with emphasis on causality, the ground plan is a plot, and the characters are ordered to acquiesce in its requirements. Except in the person of Tess (who conveys the feeling that she is greater than destiny) this aspect of his work is unsatisfactory. His characters are involved in various snares, they are finally bound hand and foot, there is ceaseless emphasis on fate, and yet, for all the sacrifices made to it, we never see the action as a living thing as we see it in *Antigone* or *Berenice* or *The Cherry Orchard*. The fate above us, not the fate working through us—that is what is eminent and memorable in the Wessex novels. (ch. v)

Although these and later remarks are compressed and sparsely illustrated, Forster appears to be saying about Hardy what might be said about his own novels. Most of them are written as ethical rather than metaphysical arguments, but they exhibit the same dogmatically imposed form which we find in the three novels[1] I have just discussed. . . .

Howards End and *A Passage to India* are also examples of novels which subordinate plausible action and psychology to an ideological pattern, but I do not wish to ventilate these matters at length since they are discussed by Frederick Crews, in his book, *E. M. Forster: The Perils of Humanism,* and argued in a detail more appropriate to

From The Appropriate Form: An Essay on the Novel *by Barbara Hardy (London: The Athlone Press, 1964), pp. 73, 75–82. Copyright © 1964 by Barbara Hardy. Reprinted by permission of the publisher. This extract is from a chapter dealing with Defoe, Charlotte Brontë, Hardy, and Forster.*

[1] [I.e., *Robinson Crusoe, Jane Eyre,* and *Jude the Obscure.*]

a full-length study of Forster.[2] I will give only a few examples of the
ideological structure of these novels. The Providential symbolism of
Mrs. Wilcox, in *Howards End,* functions in much the same way as
the figure of Old Father Time, though she is both a more central
and a more shadowy figure. She is the symbol of tradition, a special
kind of domesticated earth-goddess who is created by fantasy and made
to intervene through fantastic machinery. She leaves the house to
Margaret Schlegel, and though her family disregards her wish, Margaret becomes the mistress of Howards End. After death, she works
through the agency of her familiar Miss Avery, who moves the
Schlegel's furniture into the house and indirectly causes the breaking of Charles and Henry Wilcox. Mr. Chase might see it, with
some justification, as another instance of myth domesticated, with
the repetition of Charlotte Brontë's motif of emasculation. Mrs.
Wilcox is the strongest source of hope for the threatened community,
but her function throughout seems to be created by fantasy unbacked
by moral action. It is true that the first thing we see her do is intervene with quiet tact after Helen's encounter with Paul, but this is a
small instance of elementary common sense and sensibility and will
hardly compensate for her passivity and vagueness in the rest of the
novel. She silently devalues Margaret's intellectual friends when she
comes to visit the sisters, but this can cut both ways for readers not
wholly sympathetic to middle-class mother-figures. Her dramatic identity is mainly symbolic, unlike that of another image of heroic or-
dinariness, Leopold Bloom. Bloom is also given symbolic generalization as a modern Ulysses and perhaps a Christ figure, but he is still
shown as an ordinary good man, and it is in his moral acts and individual feelings that he provokes the sympathy which makes ethical
examples live. Mrs. Wilcox has much in common with Mrs. Ramsay,
in Virginia Woolf's *To the Lighthouse,* yet another wife-and-mother
figure who is given an apotheosis not fully endorsed by what she says
and does. In *To the Lighthouse* we also meet again the Bloomsbury
evaluation of beauty, which gives Mrs. Ramsay another dimension
which is stated but not dramatized. I cannot help feeling that both
Forster and Virginia Woolf overrate the aesthetic qualities of human
beings and relationships in a way which Henry James, as aesthetic a
novelist as either, never did. James never creates inflated valuations
of female virtue and beauty which depend heavily on the reading of
striking moral significance into rudimentary hospitality and basic

[2] [See this volume, pp. 78–89.]

maternal feeling. Both Mrs. Wilcox and Mrs. Ramsay have a fatal resemblance to Mrs. Dale and a significant lack of resemblance to the Wife of Bath and Molly Bloom. Both are interesting asexual portraits.

This is not just a matter of preferring sexual vitality and lower-class mother love. In Mrs. Moore in *A Passage to India* Forster creates a character who also depends on symbolic stature and fantastic action but whose virtues are properly enacted, so that we respond not to an idea but to an individual portrait. She is shown in action and change, and Forster makes sparing use of the *ex officio* virtues of maternity and no use at all of the aura of beauty. Mrs. Moore is convincingly detached and irritable in her relations with her son Ronnie and Adela even before she goes into the Marabar cave for her experience of vastation. She is given something of the traditional aura of age but this is combined with a realistic rendering of fatigue, techiness, and self-centredness. Her wisdom is unmysterious good plain common sense. Her virtues are simply shown, beginning with the humanity and courtesy she shows in the early encounter with Aziz at the mosque. If Leopold Bloom's virtue is compassion, also shown in action, Mrs. Moore's is a consistent respect for other creatures, whether it is for the God of the mosque, for Aziz, whom she does not think of describing immediately as an Indian, or for the wasp. Both Bloom's compassion and Mrs. Moore's respect may be called aspects of love. Mrs. Moore loses her Christian feeling in the annihilating echo of the cave, and leaves Chandrapore in impatience and detachment, both characteristics developing consistently from what we have seen of her before. Both during her life and after it she, like Mrs. Wilcox and Mrs. Ramsay, is given a supernatural power: she identifies the ghost that causes the accident, and also tells Adela that it was not Aziz who was guilty, speaking on both occasions in an unconscious trance-like manner. But she is given the substance of moral action and vivid personality. The continuity of values in her two odd children is one of Forster's more successful codas, for they exist in her shadow, standing outside the world of doubt and common experience where Fielding, knowing that his wife knows more than he can understand, is separated from Aziz as their horses swerve apart in the last lines of the novel in the final image of frail human relationships.

Frederick Crews sees the novel as sceptical and pessimistic (chap. 10). He reminds us of Forster's "disbelief in Providence" and suggests the sympathetic treatment of Hinduism is there in order to discredit the Christian and Moslem emphasis on personality: "the vastness and confusion of India are unsuitable for an orderly, benevolent deity whose attention to individuals is tireless." Hinduism, Islam, and Christianity, he concludes, are "powerless before the nihilistic message of the Marabar Caves." He seems to see this nihilistic message as final in its effects on Mrs. Moore for he speaks of her adjusting "her whole view of life to accord with the annihilation of value" and says that Adela, "unlike Mrs. Moore . . . lacks the imagination to be permanently shattered by her irrational experience." I find this implication especially puzzling since Crews admits that the last words of India to Mrs. Moore—"So you thought an echo was India; you took the Marabar Caves as final?"—affirm that the Caves "have not brought us into the presence of ultimate truth."

I suggest that Forster is pushing his intransigent material as far as he can in the direction of optimistic hope. The antivision is chiefly there, it seems to me, so that it shall be powerfully withdrawn, both for Mrs. Moore and for Adela. Mrs. Moore leaves Chandrapore and begins to revise her anti-vision. She faces a landscape less melancholy than the plain, and the houses built by man "for himself and God" strike her as "indestructible" and "appeared to her not in terms of her own trouble but as things to see." Instead of wanting to leave she longs to stay, and stands looking in the heat, fatally. She dies on leaving Bombay, after the rejection of the echo.

Crews appears to overlook these aspects of the fantastic machinery of the novel, perhaps because they are difficult to reconcile with the pessimistic suggestions which he sees as characteristic of Forster's last novel, perhaps because of their muted tentativeness. When Mrs. Moore's rejection of the echo is swiftly followed by Adela's rejection and return to sanity at the trial, we may wish to talk literally about Mrs. Moore's influence or metaphorically about her spirit. I suggest that Forster is providing us with the possibility of a miracle-working Mrs. Moore, and that he prepares for this earlier on when Mrs. Moore suggests that the accident in the car was caused by a ghost. Crews says at one point that Forster is blocking off meaning from the reader as well as from the characters, but this is not always true. He lets Mrs. Moore speak of the ghost, and then carefully tells the reader, not the characters, that this fits the facts, showing us that it is certainly how the Nawab Bahadur sees the incident. At the end, when Godbole brackets Mrs. Moore and the wasp, it is only the reader who has seen Mrs. Moore bless the wasp. Forster is elsewhere so conscious of the

uses of fantasy that it seems as if he wants to incorporate some supernatural suggestion. This is most important, and least definite, at the
trial.

Forster is very careful to tell us exactly when Mrs. Moore died,
after leaving Bombay and before reaching Aden. Ronnie tells us at
the trial that the boat should have reached Aden. This careful time-
tabling, taken in connection with the two pieces of supernatural
evidence in the ghost and the wasp, suggests that Forster wishes to indicate the possibility of Mrs. Moore transmitting her rejection of the
Caves to Adela. She is made available for "haunting" and the language used for Adela's new vision is at times religious. The vision
commences when Mrs. Moore is invoked, and when the chanting
stopped, we are told "It was as if the prayer had been heard, and the
relics exhibited." Adela's vision is not just the necessary vision of
truth, but a total reversion, involving a vision of beauty. She is not
restored to her old self but possessed by an experience which is
temporary, though some of its effects are lasting: "A new and unknown sensation protected her, like magnificent armour," "smoothly
the voice in the distance proceeded, leading along the paths of truth,"
"something caused her to add," and "though the vision was over,
and she had returned to the insipidity of the world, she remembered
what she had learnt. Atonement and confession—they could wait."
The language expresses a sense of protection and possession.

Later she thinks Fielding is speaking literally when he uses the
word exorcism, and the talk turns to ghosts and Mrs. Moore. They
join in the "fear" that the dead do not live again. This fear, and
Fielding's later assertion of his disbelief in Providence, as against
Hamidullah's belief, brings out the evidence plainly provided for the
reader and also the evidence which is withheld from the characters.
I suggest that Forster deliberately builds up a supernatural status for
Mrs. Moore, and that even if we decide to reject a Providential interpretation of Adela's confession, the question is at least raised,
and the possibility canvassed. The details of the ghost and the wasp
are suggestions leaking through the crannies of realism. I do not think
that Forster is smuggling in a Christian optimism, but that he is
creating a sense of mystery which sets up obstacles to a sceptical reading. We may interpret the vision of Adela as the benevolent haunting
of Mrs. Moore which provides the main action with its solution. Mrs.
Moore's loving respect for individuals saves Aziz and Adela. The
events which are mysterious or ambiguous suggest that love may be
powerful, even if we do not go so far as to say that God is love. And

the Hindu apotheosis is appropriate rather than ironical, or provides irony to criticize sects, not beliefs and visions. Forster revalues his humanism in a landscape and a society where the visions of beauty and love are obscure or hard to find, but he is still using symbolic short-cut and fantasy in order to make India more manageable, or at least to suggest possible grounds for faith in order. This is a much more complex ideological form than *Robinson Crusoe* or *Jane Eyre* but its schematic use of events and characters places it with them as a novel given shape by belief. Perhaps the pressure towards order is its weakness. A ghost's suggestion of hope or mystery is a fragile and whimsical use of the little gods in a novel about the great ones. So much of the material sustains the hardest look at the worst that this mystery seems manufactured, disrupting the truthfulness which is art's reflection of things as they are as well as being life's acceptance of things as they are. Moreover, the strength of Mrs. Moore lies in her power of love, her respect for the individual, and the addition of a supernatural status seems a descent rather than an ascent. Nevertheless, even if we marvel at Forster's inability to resist fantasy, even in *A Passage to India,* the novel as a whole is larger and truer than its moments of convenient fantasy. And the fantasy itself makes its hints so gently that it can be overlooked.

I began by saying that an ethical pattern of belief can determine the form of the novel, and not always without distortion, as we may see in *Lady Chatterley.* Moral categories are common to most novelists, but a rigid religious dogmatism is not, and Georg Lukacs has gone so far as to suggest that the modern novel depends on secularized values and individual responsibility. Religious ideology imposes a special structure of beneficent action and directed character, and usually involves some dramatization of the invisible world which shapes itself in symbolism and fantasy. The religious novel need not dramatize Heaven. William Golding, even where he invokes the presence of God, as in *Pincher Martin,* is writing religious fables about the Fall, not about Providence, and his actual instances of sin are not specialized but recognizeable within most ethical codes. His action and characters are not ideologically distorted. The same is true of the better and later novels of Graham Greene, amongst which *The End of the Affair* stands out as an embarrassingly distorted Providence novel. Richardson's *Pamela* is a fascinating specimen which I have excluded as a Providence novel where the flaws are certainly not simply the product of the Providential pattern. The novels I have discussed have in common either a faith or a lack of faith which involves an active demonstration of a beneficent or metaphorically malignant intervention. Both action and dramatic psychology are accordingly limited. I should end by emphasizing once more that the form of these novels cannot be reductively equated with the form of their metaphysical fables, but that the pressure of ideology affects the form in certain common ways. The common formal features which I have isolated are the more marked because of the striking individual differences. Lawrence said that Hardy's "form is execrable" because of "his clumsy efforts to push events into line with his theory of being" but saw that "his feeling, his instinct, his sensuous understanding" could fortunately work "apart from his metaphysic" (*Selected Literary Criticism*, p. 189). All the novelists I have taken to illustrate dogmatic form, attempt, with unfortunate results, to do what Lawrence calls applying the world to their metaphysic, but they are all happily incapable of doing this consistently. At times they apply the metaphysic to the world which breaks or enlarges the scheme and makes the novel more than a treatise or a fable.

Forster's "Wobblings": The Manuscripts of *A Passage to India*

by Oliver Stallybrass

E. M. Forster once referred to the "satisfaction" with which "experts in psychology, and collectors, and researchers into the process of creation" regard the "wobblings of authors" as exhibited in their manuscripts.[1] These people, or those of them within striking distance of Austin, Texas, have since 1960 been able to extend their satisfaction to Forster's own "wobblings"; for in that year the Humanities Research Center at the University of Texas acquired from the London Library all the extant manuscripts of *A Passage to India*. Since 1965 some of this satisfaction has been available also to anybody with the patience to unravel Robert L. Harrison's ingeniously tangled skein of *textus receptus* and manuscript variants.[2]

This account of the manuscripts may appropriately start with the circumstances in which they crossed the Atlantic. In 1960 the London Library, faced with acute financial difficulties, hit on the idea of an auction sale, all the objects to be sold being specially presented by members and well-wishers of the Library. E. M. Forster had been a life member since 1904 and a committee member from 1933 to 1948,

---

[1] *The Library*, series 5, vol. XIII (1958), pp. 142–3. Forster was reviewing *Authors at Work: an address delivered by Robert H. Taylor at the opening of an exhibition of literary manuscripts at the Grolier Club together with a catalogue of the exhibition by Herman W. Liebert and facsimiles of many of the exhibits* (New York, 1957).

[2] *The Manuscripts of* A Passage to India (University Microfilms, Ann Arbor, Mich., 1965), referred to in this essay as MPI.

and had once described the Library as catering "neither for the goose
nor for the rat, but for creatures who are trying to be human. The
desire to know more, the desire to feel more, and, accompanying
these but not strangling them, the desire to help others: here, briefly,
is the human aim, and the Library exists to further it." (TC, 313–14.)[3]
Now he underlined these memorable words by presenting the manuscripts of his masterpiece. They formed the sale's *pièce de résistance,*
and at £6,500 established a new record price for a manuscript by a
living author.

At that time I happened to be Chief Cataloguer at the London
Library; but my cataloguing activities were restricted, during one
of the happiest months of my life, to producing the draft of a single
entry for the Christie sale catalogue. This rate of progress is not
quite as reprehensible as it may seem: the more than 500 pieces of
paper of all shapes and sizes arrived in no discernible order, often
had totally unrelated matter on their two sides, and altogether formed
a gigantic jigsaw puzzle, some of whose pieces, Forster suggested in a
letter, "you may feel tempted to lose." Piety prevailed, however, and
only two blank pieces of paper and a few rusty paper-clips were discarded.

As publicity for the sale I had been encouraged to write a news-
paper article on the manuscripts, and this appeared in *The Guardian,*
20 June 1960. In writing it I assembled much more material than
I was able to incorporate in 1,000 words, and it is this material,
checked and revised in the light of Harrison's indispensable work,
which forms the basis of the present essay. The only other published account of the manuscripts, apparently, apart from Harrison's
own Introduction with its chapter-by-chapter commentary, is an ap-
pendix in George H. Thomson's *The Fiction of E. M. Forster.*[4] This
is a valuable study, but its emphases are closely related to a particular
interpretation of the novel, and there is room for a more general account of the manuscripts.

I use the plural advisedly: for the first fact to emerge clearly, when

---

[3] [The following abbreviations are used in the essay: TC—*Two Cheers for Democracy* (1951); HD—*The Hill of Devi* (1953); AH—*Abinger Harvest* (Pocket Ed.,
1953); HE—*Howards End* (Pocket Ed., 1947); all published by Edward Arnold and
Co.; and PI—*A Passage to India* (see n. 9 for edition used).]

[4] Wayne State University Press, Detroit, 1967, pp. 261–72. John Colmer has also
made use of the manuscripts, or rather of Harrison's edition of them, in *E. M.
Forster: A Passage to India* (Arnold, London, 1967).

I began my sorting operations, was that I was dealing not only with the "final" manuscript, but with a large quantity of earlier draft material as well. The second discovery was the need for those quotation marks round "final." The word has to be used, since Forster insists that there was no later manuscript; but it blurs the remarkable divergence between the manuscripts and the published version, between the jigsaw puzzle and the picture on the lid.

There were, in these circumstances, at least two possible assembly methods open to me. The one I chose was to start by assembling a version which should be (*a*) as complete and (*b*) as late, i.e. as close to the published text, as possible. In most cases there was no conflict between these two aims; but occasionally I had to use my judgement in assigning priority to one or the other. Thus, where an accidental gap of a mere three words could be avoided only by substituting an earlier version of the page in question, it seemed reasonable to accept the tiny gap; where, on the other hand, two consecutive pages of the generally latest version included, on the back of one, a later draft of one sentence of the other, it would have been absurd to reject a complete page for the sake of one sentence.

At the end of this stage I had assembled a version of the novel which, though written (as we shall see) over a decade and containing some inconsistencies, notably over names, is virtually continuous and complete. Many passages present in the published version are absent there—and vice versa—but of definite lacunae there are only six, all minor ones. Three are caused by the loss of, probably, one leaf in each case, and two by the imperfect dovetailing of an interpolated passage; while the sixth, already mentioned, represents a mere three words inadvertently omitted in rewriting.

Physically, this version consists of 399 single leaves, mostly folio or double folio torn in two—though sixty-six leaves have been reduced to a variety of sizes by the author's habit of tearing off, usually at the bottom, material which has been rewritten on another leaf. It is important to note that Forster, in this novel at any rate, never continues on the verso of a leaf, but always on a new recto. Nevertheless, eighty of these 399 leaves bear some writing on their versos. In a very few cases a passage has been written on a verso for interpolation in the following recto; in a few others a verso contains a *later version* of part of the following recto; and a few versos contain working notes or even, occasionally, extraneous matter, such as two fragments (MPI, 725) of what Forster has identified as abortive attempts at short stories, and also, rather curiously, a transcription of the final dialogue passage from Lawrence's *Women in Love* (MPI, 724–5).[5] The great majority, however, of these eighty used versos contain discarded draft material, sometimes deleted, sometimes not. In most cases these early drafts on what are now to be regarded as versos relate to the same general area of the book as their rectos, though there are some notable exceptions (e.g. MPI, 452–3).

It will make for ease of reference if I adopt the terms used by the Humanities Research Center and by Harrison (both of whom appear to have found my classification acceptable),[6] and refer to the main manuscript, just described, as MS. A. MS. B is the name given to the 101 remaining folio manuscripts leaves, including nineteen with versos utilised, which represent in the main variants of passages found in the rectos, and sometimes also the versos, of MS. A. Between MS. B and the versos of MS. A there seems to be no radical distinction —merely the fortuitous one of which discarded leaves came to Forster's hand, and at what stage. Indeed, one continuous fragment (MPI, 693–7) consists of A387v, B97, A388v, A393v, and B98, and illustrates neatly the problem of classification and the value of Harrison's work in reuniting fragments which I was forced to sunder.

With MS. B my method was to assemble the longest possible continuous passages, and arrange these in the order of their starting-points, in so far as I could determine these with any precision in relation either to MS. A or to the published book. No doubt some of my decisions were arbitrary, and in at least one case (B11; MPI 244–5) mistaken; in another (B59; MPI, 239 and 328–9) it looks as if at some stage a leaf has got turned over so that as regards its "recto," though not its "verso," it is badly misplaced.

In addition to the manuscripts proper there is a typescript carbon of nineteen quarto sheets known as MS. C. This includes a discarded epigraph to Part I,[7] but consists mainly of a version, intermediate

[5] Though I should not have needed help over this identification, I am in fact indebted for it to Elizabeth Heine of the University of Hawaii.

[6] Harrison, indeed, appears to endow MS. A with a more unitary status than it possesses when he suggests that "the direction of the book was fairly well established at the time of writing MS. A" (MPI, xix). I return later to the complicated question of chronology.

[7] The epigraph, of which another version is found on A32v, reads:
Four men went to pray.
The first said to the Muezzin, "Surely it is not the hour for prayer yet?"
The second said to the first, "Do not blame the Muezzin."

between MS. A and the published book, of various passages, the longest being from Chapter XXXVI;[8] also a typescript half-title page with autograph dedication, and a handwritten title-page which is clearly related to the typescript, and of which I shall have more to say. Finally there are four folded double folio leaves of corrections and addenda, to which likewise I shall return.

As we have seen, a feature of the version represented by the rectos of MS. A in their final state (and *a fortiori* of earlier versions) is its wide divergence from the published text. Chapter XXXII is unique in diverging only by one word, while a few others, notably I and XXVII–XXXI, offer only minor variants. Elsewhere, not only do the division and even the order of chapters vary—in MS. A Chapter VII precedes Chapters V and VI—but the entire text shows so many changes that but for Forster's statement to the contrary it would be tempting to postulate a later manuscript version between this one and the author's typescript, which seems to have constituted the final copy.

Instead, Forster must have made extensive alterations, either in producing the typescript, or on the typescript, or both. There are, in fact, several pieces of evidence which between them show clearly that he did both: the state of a number of the typescript leaves; the four leaves containing notes, some precise, others less so ("the whole of this Ch [i.e. XIII] . . . is not quite right"), of alterations, made or about to be made, on the numbered typescript pages; and those places (MPI, 4, for example) where, it seems, Forster grew dissatisfied while typing a page, and redrafted a sentence or two on the preceding verso. That he also retyped some leaves from a corrected carbon copy, and sent the new leaves to the publisher at a late stage, is suggested by two typescript leaves of MS. C which, though different from the book, have evidently been in the hands of the publisher or even of the printer; and this hypothesis is confirmed by other evidence, for which I am indebted to Mr. B. W. Fagan, among the records of the London publisher, Edward Arnold. Yet another indication of the complex operations involved in the production of this novel is the handwritten title-page (MS. C), the joint work of author and pub-

---

The third said to the second, "Do not blame him for blaming the Muezzin."
The fourth said, "Thank God, I am not as these other three."
The prayers of all four were unheard.

Jalaluddin Rumi

[8] Chapter numbers refer to the published book, not the manuscripts.

lisher, bearing a pencilled note in the author's hand: *"Uncorrected Typescript.* N.B. *Edith* Quested becomes *Adela* about page 40. *Khan Bahadur Nawab* Bahadur in Ch XX"*—a note which suggests, among other things, that the earlier chapters were probably typed out before the later ones were written.

This leads to the question of chronology. The author stated at one point "Green ink chapters written *c.* 1913. Adela as Edith or Janet. Ronnie [*sic*] as Gerald. Rest written 1922–1923," but later agreed that this description is not quite accurate. First, Ronny Heaslop, while his surname varies, nowhere appears as Gerald. . . . Second, the last page of the manuscript is dated January 21st, 1924. Finally, the green-ink-black-ink distinction needs modifying. The chapters written entirely or substantially in green ink are I–VII (Chapter II having in black ink eight octavo leaves evidently written at the same period as the rest, and one short interpolated passage); in addition there are green-ink leaves in the main manuscript of Chapter XII, and among the supplementary material for Chapters VIII, XII and XIV. Now, it seems unlikely that after a decade the author should again have been using green ink, but spasmodically this time instead of consistently. On the other hand, parts at least of the manuscript of Chapter VIII, being based on a story about an animal charging a car which the author heard during his second visit to India in 1921[9] (the first had been in 1912–13), must date from the later period. Graphology might settle the question, but other evidence—watermarks, the political flavour of a paragraph in Chapter IX (PI, 111), and the appearance in Chapter VIII, for the first time and in full measure, of truncated leaves[10]—suggest that it would be more correct to say "Chapter I–VII and subsequent green-ink leaves written *c.* 1913, rest written 1922 or 1923 to 1924." In this case, eleven leaves are all that remain of the earlier version for Chapters VIII–XIV; though it is possible that Chapters IX–XI, which are not essential from a structural point of view, had no existence until the later period. The interesting points in any case are the long interval, and the fact that each creative period followed a visit to India.

Apart from a few pages which are evidently fair copies, the manu-

---

[9] See PI, Everyman's Library ed., Dent, London, repr. 1957, p. xxix; and HD, 89–90.

[10] This habit of decapitating (or more commonly depeditating) partially rewritten leaves, in order to use the versos of the discarded segments, may have been acquired under wartime conditions in Egypt; the late H. E. Wortham, who edited the *Egyptian Mail* at the time, told me that Forster's contributions were often written on the backs of envelopes.

scripts are untidy. Mention has already been made of the various sizes to which many leaves have been reduced. Sometimes the matter discarded in this way has first been deleted, sometimes not, and, since the tear is often roughly made, occasional undeleted but redundant words are to be found. There is much deletion and correction, some of it in pencil, and, to quote the author again, "scriggles . . . surge up from the margin, they extend tentacles, they interbreed." [11] Apart from "scriggles," the margins contain occasional dates (unreliable: two consecutive dates in Chapter XX read 9/7/23 and 10/6/23), tallies of words, and question marks, some of which suggest factual points to be verified, others perhaps a vague dissatisfaction. A few chapters have their pages numbered in pencil, but the majority have only what appears to be an indication of how many pages they contain, or once contained, while the numbering of the chapters themselves is erratic and shows traces of alteration, some of it done by the author immediately before delivery to the London Library. As for the actual handwriting, this undoubtedly comes into the category of "cacography if there is such a word." [11] (There is.)

The main impression conveyed by the manuscripts, and by their divergences from the book, is of an author who writes fast, and uses the physical act of writing as part of "the process of creation," not as a mere recording technique. Speed would account for some curious spelling mistakes and for such slips as "service" for "surface," "break" for "brake," "their" for "there," and "parents' pupils" for "pupils' parents" (MPI, 79)—this last, it is amusing to note, occurring in three other fragments (MPI, 39, 40, 42) as a deliberately introduced slip of the tongue. It is fascinating to compare these first and final versions— some passages have as many as five drafts—and to see a touch of irony added, a wrong note eliminated, an inert snatch of dialogue springing suddenly to life. An author's "improvements" are not always accepted as such by all his readers—Henry James is a case in point— but few are likely to quarrel with the judgement revealed in the following changes:

". . . Mrs. Turton takes bribes, red-nose is apparently still a bachelor." (MPI, 8.)
". . . *Mrs. Turton takes bribes, Mrs. Red-nose does not and cannot, because so far there is no Mrs. Red-nose.*" (PI, 13.)

. . . a family marriage that had been celebrated with imperfect solemnity. (MPI, 12.)

[11] *The Library, loc. cit.*

. . . *a family circumcision that had been celebrated with imperfect pomp.* (PI, 15.)[12]

". . . the verandah is good enough for an Indian and Mrs. Callander takes my carriage and cuts me dead. . . ." (MPI, 28; Aziz is speaking.)
". . . *the verandah is good enough for an Indian, yes, yes, let him stand, and Mrs. Callendar takes my carriage and cuts me dead. . . ."* (PI, 25.)

. . . in case the natives should see the Englishwomen acting. . . . (MPI, 35.)
. . . *lest the servants should see their mem-sahibs acting. . . .* (PI, 26.)

One touch of regret—not conversational regret, but the stab that goes down to the soul—would have made him a different man, and she would have worshipped him. (MPI, 89.)
One touch of regret—not the canny substitute but the true regret from the heart—would have made him a different man, and the British Empire a different institution. (PI, 54.)

He was inaccurate because he desired to honour her. (MPI, 343.)
He was inaccurate because he desired to honour her, and—facts being entangled—he had to arrange them in her vicinity, as one tidies the ground after extracting a weed. (PI, 165.)

. . . he chose to pretend that Mr. Das had a sense of justice equal to his own. (MPI, 471.)
. . . *he liked to maintain that his old Das really did possess moral courage of the Public School brand.* (PI, 224.)

Her particular brand of sensations and opinions—why should they claim so much importance in the world? (MPI, 476.)
Her particular brand of opinions, and the surburban Jehovah who sanctified them—by what right did they claim so much importance in the world, and assume the title of civilisation? (PI, 226-7.)

One could multiply such examples endlessly. In addition, there is a general tendency to convert narrative into dialogue—though occasionally the reverse happens, as when "a shapeless discussion occurred" (PI, 47) replaces the actual discussion (MPI, 72)—and to eliminate explanatory comment of the "he was lying" type (MPI, 607). Some passages in the book—including the famous jest about the "pinko-grey" races (PI, 66) and the speech of Aziz about the need of

---

[12] This alteration may reflect the difference between what was felt mentionable in print in 1913 and in 1923; just as the omission, on which Forster himself has commented (AH, 173-4), from the second edition of *Sense and Sensibility* of a sentence containing the words "natural daughter" reflected a change in the opposite direction.

Indians for "kindness, more kindness, and even after that more kindness" (PI, 122)—are absent from the manuscripts; while the latter contain much material that was finally rejected. Forster's admirers are likely to relish many such passages as the account of Fielding's past (MPI, 107-9), that of the chauffeur's origins (MPI, 168), and the rumours of Adela's death: "By four o'clock Adela was dead or dying all over the Civil Station and as far as the Railway. North of the railway she was known to be ill . . . ." (MPI, 395). They may even be tempted to feel that too many babies have gone out with the bathwater; but in most cases they will probably agree that the interests of economy and form have rightly prevailed.

Some of the changes affect the characterisation perceptibly. Aziz appears to have been observed with almost complete clarity from the outset, but Fielding would have been a subtly different person if he had been allowed to retain his motor-bicycle (MPI, 219), to smoke cigarettes instead of a pipe (MPI, 409; PI, 194), and to practise the characteristic Wilcox ritual of looking at his watch (MPI, 79; cf. HE, 107, 201, 222, 232). Adela (alias Violet, alias Janet, alias Edith) is more aggressive in the earlier manuscript chapters—"she had little self-control and had learnt[13] at Cambridge that one ought to show when one's bored" (MPI, 82)—more like the suffragette *manquée* of the 1960 London stage production. Other examples are noted by Harrison.

Inconsistencies of name are not without significance: at one stage Ronny bore the surname Moore, which, combined with other evidence, suggests that at that period Part III of the novel had not been projected. The numbering and renumbering of chapters have already been mentioned, and have their own interest: one most effective change, isolating and emphasising as it does the almost personal power of the climate, is the renumbering of what was originally a single chapter as the present Chapters IX, X, and XI.

Turning to more obvious structural issues, we find in almost every chapter variants of incident: both the engagement and its rupture, for example, are treated very differently in the manuscripts, so is the "bridge party," so is the trial; above all, so is the expedition to the Marabar caves. It is an interesting fact that, of the 101 leaves of MS. B, no less than fifty-five represent earlier drafts of Chapters XIV–XVI, and it is clear that this central episode caused the author an unusual amount of trouble; it seems probable, indeed, that this is

[13] Perhaps from Stewart Ansell.

one reason why the book was not completed around 1913. (Another may have been the need to refresh his memory of Indian English.) These drafts vary greatly from each other and from the book. In one version (MPI, 310) the famous account of the echo is given in the form of a dialogue, in the first cave, between Aziz and Adela (Edith); in another (MPI, 337–8) the echo is linked with Fielding's reflections, not Mrs. Moore's, and it is Fielding, not Aziz, who finds the field-glasses, while the two men have apparently been acquainted long enough for Aziz to have "compelled" Fielding to learn the four lines of Persian poetry which are quoted in Chapter II (PI, 22) but are not in MS. A at that point. Some of the writing illustrates well the modest beginnings from which so much of the impressive final version emerges: in one early four-leaf draft Adela, in a supposedly hysterical state, is actually made to say something as wooden and unconvincing as "Miss Derek, I have been lacking in sympathy myself all my life, I feel." (MPI, 316.)

This fragment of four leaves is perhaps the most intriguing in the entire trove, for it answers unequivocally the question which, *pace* the confident conclusions of some critics, the author has so scrupulously refrained from answering in the book: whether (ignoring the more implausible explanations) Adela was the victim of halluci-nation or of attempted assault by somebody other than Aziz. In this early stage of the book's genesis, at least, there *was* an assault (MPI, 315); as is confirmed elsewhere in some working notes headed "Situ-ation at the catastrophe" (MPI, 723). This is one of a number of notes scattered around the versos and margins, of which two others may be mentioned as examples of the light they shed on the author's discarded intentions and his methods: the remarkable "Aziz & Janet drift into one another's arms—then apart" (MPI, 722), and the mar-ginal note against McBryde's appearance in Chapter XVIII, "Intro-duce him earlier" (MPI, 364)—as is duly done in Chapter V of the book.

Finally the manuscripts shed light on one or two doubtful read-ings in the published texts. The curious use of "draggled" (PI, 220) in the apparent sense of "tangled," is confirmed (MPI, 464), as is the substantival use of "beat up" (PI, 275; MPI, 588) where "heat up" might have been expected—though this may be one of those slips of the pen to which I have referred. On the other hand, future editions of *A Passage to India* will surely have to correct "Others praised Him without attributes" (PI, 327) to ". . . with attributes" (MPI, 698), "half dead" (PI, 331) to "half deaf" (MPI, 706), and "fifty five-hundred"

(PI, 335; MPI, 716) to the reading from MS. B, "fifty or five-hundred" (MPI, 717).[14]

The paramount interest of the manuscripts, however, is the remarkable light they throw on "the process of creation" and on one of the great English novels; and I cannot end this essay without expressing the hope that other manuscripts of the same author will one day enter the public domain.

[14] For drawing my attention to all these points I am indebted to George H. Thomson. In the last example the actual reading of MS. B. is "50 or 500."

Chronology of Important Dates

	Forster	The Age
1879	January 1: Edward Morgan Forster born in London.	
1888		Kipling, *Plain Tales from the Hills.*
1891		Kipling, *Life's Handicap.*
1897–1901	Attended King's College, Cambridge.	Olive Schreiner, *Trooper Peter Halket of Mashonaland* (1897); Kipling, *The Day's Work* (1898), *Kim* (1901). The Boer War (1899–1901).
1901–2	Travelled in Greece and Italy.	Conrad, *Heart of Darkness* (1902; first published 1899 in *Blackwood's Magazine*).
1903		Butler, *The Way of All Flesh;* G. E. Moore, *Principia Ethica.*
1904		Conrad, *Nostromo.*
1905	*Where Angels Fear to Tread.*	Wells, *Kipps.*
1906		Galsworthy, *The Man of Property.*
1907	*The Longest Journey.*	Shaw, *John Bull's Other Island.*
1908	*A Room with a View.*	
1909		Passage of the Morley–Minto reforms, designed to secure an extension of representative institutions in India.
1910	*Howards End.*	
1911	*The Celestial Omnibus* (short stories).	
1912–13	Visited India for the first time and began work on *A Passage to India.*	
1914–18	Served in Alexandria in the	World War I. Lawrence, *The*

	course of the war as voluntary Red Cross worker.	*Rainbow* (1915); Woolf, *The Voyage Out* (1915); Joyce, *A Portrait of the Artist as a Young Man* (1916); Eliot, *Prufrock and Other Observations* (1917); Strachey, *Eminent Victorians* (1918).
1919		Further constitutional reforms in India. The "Amritsar Massacre."
1920	Literary editor of *The Daily Herald*.	Lawrence, *Women in Love;* Lewis, *Main Street.*
1921	March–November: Visited India for the second time, as Private Secretary to the Maharajah of Dewas State Senior.	
1922	*Alexandria: A History and a Guide.*	Eliot, *The Waste Land;* Galsworthy, *The Forsyte Saga;* Joyce, *Ulysses;* Lewis, *Babbitt;* Woolf, *Jacob's Room.*
1923	*Pharos and Pharillon* (literary and historical sketches).	Huxley, *Antic Hay.*
1924	*A Passage to India.*	Shaw, *St. Joan;* Melville, *Billy Budd.*
1925		Woolf, *Mrs. Dalloway;* Lawrence, *St. Mawr.*
1927	*Aspects of the Novel.*	
1928	*The Eternal Moment* (short stories).	
1934	*Goldsworthy Lowes Dickinson* (biography).	
1936	*Abinger Harvest* (essays).	
1939	*What I Believe.*	
1945	Elected Honorary Fellow of King's College, Cambridge.	
1951	*Two Cheers for Democracy* (essays).	
1953	*The Hill of Devi.*	
1954	*Collected Short Stories.*	
1956	*Marianne Thornton.*	
1970	June 7: Death of Forster.	

Notes on the Editor and Contributors

ANDREW RUTHERFORD is Regius Professor of English, University of Aberdeen, and the author of *Byron: A Critical Study* (1961) and other works. He is the editor of *Kipling's Mind and Art* (1964) and *Byron: The Critical Heritage* (1970).

NIRAD C. CHAUDHURI, man of letters, journalist, and broadcaster, is the author of *The Autobiography of an Unknown Indian* (1951), *A Passage to England* (1959), *The Continent of Circe* (1965), and other works.

C. B. COX is Professor of English, University of Manchester, and author of *The Free Spirit* (1963) and other works. He is coauthor of *Modern Poetry: Studies in Practical Criticism* (1963), editor of *Dylan Thomas: A Collection of Critical Essays* (1966), and coeditor of *The Critical Quarterly* and *T. S. Eliot: "The Waste Land": A Casebook* (1968).

FREDERICK C. CREWS, Professor of English, University of California, is the author of *The Tragedy of Manners* (1957), *E. M. Forster: The Perils of Humanism* (1962), *The Pooh Perplex* (1964), *The Sins of the Fathers: Hawthorne's Psychological Themes* (1966), and other works.

BARBARA HARDY is Professor of English, Royal Holloway College, University of London, and the author of *The Novels of George Eliot* (1959), *The Appropriate Form* (1964), and other works. She is the editor of *Middlemarch: Critical Approaches to the Novel* (1967).

WALTER A. S. KEIR, critic, broadcaster, and reviewer, is Lecturer in English, University of Aberdeen. He served in the Indian Army from 1940–45.

ARNOLD KETTLE is Professor of Literature, The Open University, and the author of *An Introduction to the English Novel* (1951–53), *Karl Marx: Founder of Modern Communism* (1963), and other works. He is the editor of *Shakespeare in a Changing World* (1964).

OLIVER STALLYBRASS, man of letters and translator of Scandinavian works, is United Kingdom Editorial Representative of Stanford University Press. He is the editor of *Aspects of E. M. Forster* (1969) and of the *Journal of the Royal Central Asian Society*.

LIONEL TRILLING, Professor of English, Columbia University, is the author of *Matthew Arnold* (1939), *E. M. Forster* (1943), *The Middle of the Journey*

(1947), *The Liberal Imagination* (1950), *The Opposing Self* (1955), *A Gathering of Fugitives* (1957), *Beyond Culture* (1966), and other works.

GERTRUDE M. WHITE is Professor of English, Oakland University, and the author of *Wilfred Owen* (1969) and other works.

Selected Bibliography

Forster's own works—his short stories, essays, reminiscences (especially *The Hill of Devi*), and other novels—provide some of the most useful glosses on *A Passage to India*.

Annals of English Literature 1475–1950, 2nd ed. (Oxford: Clarendon Press, 1961), lists the principal publications for each year, enabling the reader to see Forster's writings in the context of literary history; while a useful account of ethical and aesthetic theories current in Forster's milieu is to be found in J. K. Johnstone, *The Bloomsbury Group: A Study of E. M. Forster, Lytton Strachey, Virginia Woolf, and Their Circle* (London: Secker and Warburg Ltd., 1954).

A sympathetic and well-documented account of Anglo-India is provided by Philip Woodruff [Philip Mason] in *The Men Who Ruled India* (London: Jonathan Cape Ltd., 1953–54), especially Vol. II, *The Guardians.* For an opposing view, see V. G. Kiernan, *The Lords of Human Kind: European Attitudes to the Outside World in the Imperial Age* (London: Weidenfeld & Nicholson, 1969). K. Natwar-Singh, "Only Connect . . . : Forster and India," in Oliver Stallybrass, ed., *Aspects of E. M. Forster* (London: Edward Arnold [Publishers] Ltd., 1969), and K. Natwar-Singh, ed., *E. M. Forster: A Tribute* (New York: Harcourt, Brace & World, Inc., 1964), are of limited interest as presenting recent Indian views of Forster's personality and achievement.

Malcolm Bradbury, ed., *Forster: A Collection of Critical Essays* (Englewood Cliffs, N. J.: Prentice-Hall, Inc., 1966) is an indispensable collection of critical essays with a valuable introduction and bibliography. Other important recent studies apart from those represented in this volume include J. B. Beer, *The Achievement of E. M. Forster* (London: Chatto and Windus Ltd., 1962); Denis Godfrey, *E. M. Forster's Other Kingdom* (Edinburgh and London: Oliver and Boyd Ltd., 1968); James McConkey, *The Novels of E. M. Forster* (Ithaca, N. Y.: Cornell University Press, 1957); Wilfred Stone, *The Cave and the Mountain* (Stanford: Stanford University Press, 1966); George H. Thomson, *The Fiction of E. M. Forster* (Detroit: Wayne State University Press, 1967); and Alan Wilde, *Art and Order: A Study of E. M. Forster* (New York: New York University Press, 1964; London: Peter Owen Ltd., 1965).

TWENTIETH CENTURY
INTERPRETATIONS

MAYNARD MACK, *Series Editor*
Yale University

NOW AVAILABLE
Collections of Critical Essays
ON

ADVENTURES OF HUCKLEBERRY FINN
ALL FOR LOVE
THE AMBASSADORS
ARROWSMITH
AS YOU LIKE IT
BLEAK HOUSE
THE BOOK OF JOB
THE CASTLE
CORIOLANUS
DOCTOR FAUSTUS
DON JUAN
DUBLINERS
THE DUCHESS OF MALFI
ENDGAME
EURIPIDES' ALCESTIS
THE FALL OF THE HOUSE OF USHER
A FAREWELL TO ARMS
THE FROGS
GRAY'S ELEGY
THE GREAT GATSBY
GULLIVER'S TRAVELS
HAMLET
HARD TIMES
HENRY IV, PART ONE
HENRY IV, PART TWO
HENRY V
THE ICEMAN COMETH
JULIUS CAESAR

(continued on next page)

(*continued from previous page*)

KEATS'S ODES
LIGHT IN AUGUST
LORD JIM
MAJOR BARBARA
MEASURE FOR MEASURE
THE MERCHANT OF VENICE
MOLL FLANDERS
MUCH ADO ABOUT NOTHING
THE NIGGER OF THE "NARCISSUS"
OEDIPUS REX
THE OLD MAN AND THE SEA
PAMELA
THE PLAYBOY OF THE WESTERN WORLD
THE PORTRAIT OF A LADY
A PORTRAIT OF THE ARTIST AS A YOUNG MAN
THE PRAISE OF FOLLY
PRIDE AND PREJUDICE
THE RAPE OF THE LOCK
THE RIME OF THE ANCIENT MARINER
ROBINSON CRUSOE
ROMEO AND JULIET
SAMSON AGONISTES
THE SCARLET LETTER
SIR GAWAIN AND THE GREEN KNIGHT
SONGS OF INNOCENCE AND OF EXPERIENCE
SONS AND LOVERS
THE SOUND AND THE FURY
THE TEMPEST
TESS OF THE D'URBERVILLES
TOM JONES
TO THE LIGHTHOUSE
TWELFTH NIGHT
THE TURN OF THE SCREW
UTOPIA
VANITY FAIR
WALDEN
THE WASTE LAND
WOMEN IN LOVE
WUTHERING HEIGHTS